Dark Psychology

The Secrets and Techniques of Manipulation, NLP, Body Language, Mind Control, and How to Analyze and Read People. Detect and Defend Yourself from the Manipulated

Anthony Page

Table of Contents

Introduction

Warren Jeffs, the president and prophet of the Fundamentalist Church of Jesus Christ of Latter-Day Saints, was sentenced to life plus twenty years in prison in 2011. He's famous for his polygamous ways and child brides. The man who preached that he was a prophet of God and had thousands of followers used manipulation and persuasion to get people to believe what he was teaching; which resulted in controlling all aspects of their lives and the lives of their children.

Elissa Wall was forced to become a child bride under her uncle's rule. Someone who should have been there to protect her forced her to marry her cousin at the age of 14. When she came to him in confidence after her husband sexually and physically abused her, he reminded her that she was her husband's property and he could do whatever he wanted to with her. Emma was more outspoken than most of the other girls in the sect, and because of that, Jeffs wanted to ensure her submission. Forcing her to marry her cousin and having him control her body, mind, and soul was his way of silencing her into submission.

Jeffs and other cult leaders, such as Charles Manson use power, manipulation, and control to get people to follow them. They prey on their darkest fears and desires to sucker them in, and then they never let them go.

Criminals like Jeffs, use what is known as Dark Psychology. Psychology is the study of human behavior. Psychology studies human thought, actions, and interactions. Dark Psychology falls into the same category as general psychology. However, it goes deeper into the human mind and helps pinpoint tactics that people use to motivate, persuade, manipulate, and coerce to get what they want from others.

The Dark Triad is a term in Dark Psychology that can be helpful when trying to pinpoint the beginning of criminal behavior.

- Narcissism is the exhibition of these traits: egotism, grandiosity, and lack of empathy
- Machiavellianism is the use of manipulation to betray and exploit people. Those who practice this do not follow morality or ethics.
- Psychopathy is to trick those who put their trust in these types of people. They are often charming and friendly. Yet they are ruled by impulsivity, selfishness, lack of empathy, and remorselessness.

None of us want to fall prey to manipulation, especially from those who we love. The result is that we often are. Dark Psychology tactics can be used regularly. For instance, some of them are found in commercials, or internet ads selling certain products, and can also be found when we are asked to buy something at a store, a car lot, or even in a fast-food restaurant. Some of the everyday techniques that we can experience are:

- Lying – White lies, untruths, partial or half-truths, exaggerations, and stretching the truth.

- Love flooding – Through endless compliments, affection or through what is known as "buttering someone up".
- Love denial – telling someone that they do not love you and withhold your love or affection from them until you get what you want.
- Withdrawal – through avoiding the person altogether or giving them "the silent treatment".
- Choice restriction – Giving people options that distract them from the one decision that you don't want them to make.
- Reverse psychology – Trying to get a person to do the exact opposite of what you want them to do in the attempt to motivate them to do the direct opposite, which is what you really wanted them to do in the first place.
- Semantic Manipulation – Using common words that have a mutual definition with a person and later telling them that you have a different view of the conversation that you just had.

Not everyone who uses these tactics are part of the dark triad. These tactics are usually taught to children by their parents or other influential adults in their lives. They are often learned or taught to children through watching. These are not people that you should watch out for. It is the people who used these tactics to manipulate you for their own benefit -whether it is to control you or bend you to their will. These are the type of people that you should watch out for. We will break down the components of manipulation, persuasion, deception, and brainwashing in this book and how you can avoid those who mean to do you harm.

Chapter One: The Differences Between Persuasion and Manipulation

"Manipulation is an emotionally unhealthy psychological strategy used by people who are incapable of asking for what they want and need in a direct way"

(Shortsleeve, 2019)

Manipulation is a way to control others, and it can be used in different ways. Some of these ways can be very subtle, and others can be easily recognizable, especially if you know what you are looking for.

With manipulation, one of the first things that a person will notice is the feeling of fear, obligation and/or guilt. When someone is trying to manipulate you, they are trying to coerce you to do something that you don't want to do. You feel scared thinking about doing what they want or feeling scared in the act, there is a feeling of obligation that goes along with it, and you sometimes feel guilty if you don't do it at all.

The two types of manipulators that can make you feel this way are known as a bully and a victim. When someone bullies you, they are often using fear in the form of aggression, threats, and intimidation to make you do what they want.

On the other hand, if they play the victim, they try to make you think that they are hurt. No matter the case, they are often the ones who caused the problem in the first place. If you are being targeted by a manipulator who is playing the victim, you will do whatever they want to stop their suffering. You might even feel responsible for their suffering, even though you are not.

Another thing a person who is being manipulated does is question themselves and what they are doing. This can often be referred to as gaslighting. This type of manipulation has people not only questioning themselves but what is real to them, what they perceive, their own thoughts, and even their memory. Has someone ever twisted your words around and made it about them? Have they taken over the conversation to make you feel like you're the perpetrator and that you did something wrong while you wonder what it is that you exactly did? Gaslighters know how to make their victims feel a false sense of guilt, responsibility and even defensiveness. They will have you questioning if you have done something wrong when you haven't at all.

Another manipulation tactic comes with strings attached. People should want to do things for you just because they want to and not what they can get out of it. This is one of the most common forms of manipulation. You feel like someone is being nice to you and doing things for you when you need them. But there always seems to be a catch or something involved. If you don't adhere to those stipulations, then they make you feel ungrateful, like you are taking advantage of their kindness.

There are other forms of manipulation, but these are the most common forms. It is imperative to know what manipulation is and the different forms so that you can protect yourself against it.

Manipulation is not the only control tactic that we should watch out for. Persuasion is another form of control used against people daily. Kendra Cherry (2018) defines persuasion as "a symbolic process in which communicators try to convince other people to change their attitudes or behaviors regarding an issue through the transmission of a message in an atmosphere of free choice."

Persuasion can be found in images, sounds and even through the use of words. There is a deliberate attempt to influence others. One of the key points about persuasion is that people are not coerced or manipulated; instead, they are free to choose what they believe. Even though the images, sounds or words used in advertisements help them choose what others tell them too. Persuasion can be found in advertisements or messages on radio, the internet, television, billboards, and face to face communication through verbal and non-verbal ways.

This technique has increased over the years and especially in the 21st century. Messages in the form of advertisements over different sorts of media have grown and are spread rather rapidly. On average, every U.S. adult is exposed to 300 to 3,000 advertisements every day (Cherry, 2018).

It can even be found within business itself, and we are not talking about advertising agencies. There are a lot of companies that use the art of persuasion to sell goods and services.

Many of the advertisements that we see have been specially made or crafted to get people to buy their products or services because they want to look like them or live that certain lifestyle.

If both manipulation and persuasion are prevalent in advertising, then what are their core differences?

How can you tell them apart?

"Advertising manipulates when it encourages the audience to form untrue beliefs" (Noggle, 2018). This occurs when we are told that fried chicken is healthy, or when the associations that are used are often faulty, like Marlboro cigarettes and the association with the ruggedness of the Marlboro Man. If the manipulation of the Marlboro man is successful, the ads themselves contribute to disease and death. People often think of manipulation as wrong because it harms the person being manipulated. And, this is the case most of the time. But there are times when manipulation itself is not harmful.

Immanuel Kant stated that "morality requires us to treat each other as rational beings rather than mere objects" (Noggle, 2018). The only rational way that we can even try to manipulate people, or their behavior is through rational persuasion, and any other way is just immoral and even unethical.

What makes manipulation wrong?

In any situation, the manipulator tries to get the other person to believe what the manipulator feels is wrong. The manipulator is lying to the other person, and to make the other person make some form of mistake. Thus, they can also make you believe a false statement, make you feel inappropriate, get someone else's approval in the wrong way or to doubt something, even yourself. There is no good reason to get someone to doubt. So, to answer the question above, the core distinction between manipulation and non-manipulation depends on the manipulator and if they are trying to get someone to make some sort of mistake regarding how they feel, think, doubt, or pay attention to something.

Reasonable persuasion, defined by Immanuel Kant, is the only moral way to influence people. As was stated earlier in the chapter, persuasion is something we all experience, as well as do, every single day. If it is reasonable, then it is not evil. It is just considered to be one of the ways that we interact with everyone around us. You might want to persuade someone to think a certain way because you want to see the world become a better place. This is often true when you are debating with someone about their political view of the world and you come back with an intelligent, researched argument that changes their perception. Did you harm them in any way? No, you reasonably persuaded them to come to your side. They made the choice all on their own.

Another way that you can persuade someone is through making a profit. All types of persuasion further some sort of self-interest. There is nothing wrong with making money. It isn't evil, unethical or immoral. However, you have to persuade another person to part with their money by getting them to believe that what you have to sell – whether it is a good or service – is what they want or need.

Jonathan Fields states that the difference between persuasion and manipulation can be defined in three ways:

- The intent behind the reason you want to persuade someone
- The truth behind the process
- The benefit of impact on the person you are trying to persuade

For example, Amber married Devon 2 years ago, and they started to have marital problems during the beginning of their second year of marriage. One-night Devon comes home drunk and hits Amber in the face. The abuse continues from there until one night she wakes up in the hospital with broken bones. Amber's parents are sitting beside the bed, and her mother takes her hand in hers. That night her parents urge her to leave Devon because it is in her best interest. They know she loves him, but he needs to get help for his anger. They persuade her to file domestic violence charges against him because the next time she might not be so lucky, and they can't lose their baby girl.

Now Amber has a choice in all of this. She has the choice to stay with Devon and risk that things will get better or worse. Or she has the choice to leave him with or without pressing charges. Her parent's argument was reasonably persuasive, but they were still giving her a choice. They did not force her or influence her to make a choice. There were quite a few ways, as was stated before, to manipulate the situation and make her do what they wanted, even if that wasn't what she wanted, which would be manipulation. There is no good type of manipulation, only good persuasion.

Amber isn't dumb and knows what she is risking if she goes back to Devon. And, this is where the persuasion influences her to make a choice. The argument her parents brought to her is with love and compassion. They care about her well-being, and they want her to know that she can come home, and everything will be okay. Amber feels good making this decision and is not making it out of remorse, guilt or out of obligation to her family. This is the main and very important difference between persuasion and manipulation.

This is why it is important to know the difference. When you are persuading someone, they often are feeling better for meeting you. Those who are being manipulated, feel guilt the second you leave. (Roberts, 2019).

Chapter Two: The History of Persuasion

In 1964 a political television advertisement aired during the presidential campaign. The ad only aired once, but it was so controversial, that it was considered to be an important factor in Lyndon B. Johnson's landslide victory against Barry Goldwater and is known as one of the most controversial political advertisements in television history.

The ad itself starts with a little girl, three years of age, who is in a meadow surrounded by birds. She is holding a daisy and picking apart its petals, counting each one cutely, missing or repeating numbers, even in the wrong order. She pauses at the number nine as if she is thinking about the next number and a male narrator speaks over her, saying "ten," as if he is starting a missile launch countdown. The little girl turns her head toward a point off-screen, and everything freezes after that. The narrator continues to countdown, and the screen focuses on the little girl's eye; her pupil is filling the entire screen. The screen blacks out when it reaches zero, and the viewers can hear and see the flash and sound of a nuclear explosion – which is similar to video footage of the surface burst Trinity test of the atomic bomb in 1945. The viewer is left looking at a giant mushroom cloud, and a final slow close-up view of the explosion and the destruction is left on the screen.

Next, the screen moves to the real footage of the nuclear detonation and Lyndon B. Johnson's voice is heard over it. "These are the stakes. To make a world in which all of God's children can live or go into the dark. We must either love each other, or we must die." (Nowicki, 2016). Then the footage is replaced with words written on the screen and read by another voice, "Vote for President Johnson on November 3rd The stakes are too high for you to stay home." (Nowicki, 2016). Barry Goldwater's name was not mentioned once in the entire advertisement.

The art of persuasion is over 2,000 years old, and Aristotle's *Rhetoric* is one of the earliest documents in history that discusses it. Aristotle was a Greek philosopher who was a student of Plato's. He studied and frequently wrote on metaphysics and politics, among others. His view on rhetoric was very compelling because it created long-lasting ideas about the art of persuasion and how it could be used.

Persuasion is defined as a broad term for influence. It is where a person can attempt to influence another person's beliefs, attitudes, intentions, motivations, and/or behaviors. People often use persuasion for their personal gain like election campaigning that is discussed at the beginning of the chapter, giving a sales pitch to a potential client or customer, and in trial advocacy. It can also be viewed as using one's own resources to change another person's behavior or attitude.

There are two types of persuasion:

- Systematic Persuasion - is a process where someone's attitude, behavior, or beliefs are controlled through the appeal of logic and reason.
- Heuristic Persuasion - is a process where someone's attitude, behavior, or beliefs are controlled through habit or emotion.

Ancient Greeks

"Persuasion is effected through the medium of the hearers when they shall have been brought to a state of excitement under the influence of speech; for we do not, when influenced by pain or joy, or partiality or dislike, award our decisions in the same way; about which means of persuasion alone. I declare that the system-mongers of the present-day bury themselves."

-Aristotle

Aristotle himself defined persuasion as a way to appeal to an audience through three different ways: ethos, logos, and pathos

- ***Ethos*** looks at the character of the person who is speaking because they want to appear credible. Aristotle states that there are three prerequisites for someone to appear credible: competence, good intentions, and empathy. A person can view ethos during the speaker's performance through their voice, gestures, facial expressions, proxemics, body language, and movement. How a person can determine the influencing factors of ethos is through their clothes, vocabulary, slang, as well as their social aspects like rank, popularity, etc.

  A person's reputation can affect if they influence the audience or not. You might listen to a speech given by the president because of his reputation, then his running mate who has no business or political experience. These particular factors can affect the appearance and reception of the speaker, given the situation. The speaker can use statements to position themselves, as well as reveal their social hierarchy, preferences, distastes, etc. (Ethos, Pathos, & Logos, 2019).

- ***Pathos*** looks at the emotions of the speaker and how they use them to influence their audience. Every speech given in history's goal is to persuade the audience and to bring them to the side of the speaker. One of the best ways to do this is to use their emotions against them. Aristotle said that it was highly important for each speaker to know what emotions exist, and how and/or under what circumstances could they be provoked. The speaker has several positions to provoke the emotions of their audience. However, knowing who your audience can help with the emotional persuasion.

  Some high emotional topics that speakers often reference are value and belief systems. Some techniques can be used during the presentation, like storytelling that bring the audience in. People react differently to stories, especially if you compare them to a lecture. The goal of using the pathos method is to reduce the judgment of the audience. Speakers using this type of influence use languages such as metaphor, simile, and vivid imagery to sway their audience by painting vivid pictures. They can also use emotional anecdotes and vivid connotative language that creates sympathy or emotional interest in a topic. An example of doing this is to use correct figures of speech that can be used in certain arguments or content of the argument in the fore or background because it allows the speaker to be more effective during their delivery, while underline their strengths and minimizing the weak parts of their argument (Ethos, Pathos & Logos, 2019).

- ***Logos*** look at the logic behind the argument. Logic enhances the content and argument of the speech. However, like ethos and pathos, the goal is to be as persuasive as one can to their audience. During the speech, the arguments, the argument schemes, the different forms of proof, and the reasoning are special to the interest of the argument itself. There are two forms of proof: natural and artificial. Natural proof is based on data that has been extracted from documents, testimonies, etc. Artificial proof is created through a combination of information (hints, examples, etc.), as well as the art of logic (Ethos, Pathos & Logos, 2019). For example, the speaker, in this case, will use credible facts, statistics that are related to the current topic, allusions, deductive reasoning, as well as citing credible sources or people outside of the speech itself.

Aristotle and the Ancient Greeks were the first people to show the world the importance of rhetoric, oration, persuasion, and communication within the community, democracy and within the functioning Greek City-State called the polis. The Greeks saw persuasion as something powerful and perceived it as one of the most critical aspects of human welfare and human happiness. The power to deliver a free exchange of opinions and counterarguments within the political area, guaranteed the arrival of a political consensus because everyone was able to make their own choice, and was not coerced. To live inside the polis – and to be a part of it – meant that everything was decided through words and persuasion, not through force or violence.

Rhetoric and elocution skills were expected of every politician, especially a successful one. Every single trial was held in front of the assembly. The arguments from the prosecution and the defense relied on the persuasion of each of the speakers.

That was why rhetoric was thought of so highly. It was the available means of persuasion in any situation. Aristotle gave four reasons why a person should learn the art of persuasion.

1. Truth and justice are faultless principles. Therefore, if a speaker loses a case, then it is the fault of that speaker.

2. Persuasion is an excellent tool for teaching how to argue.

3. A good speaker or rhetorician needs to know the argument on both sides. This way, they will have a solid argument and understand the whole problem, as well as all of the options.

4. The art of persuasion is one of the best ways to defend yourself.

Persuasion has thrived throughout the centuries. Good leaders used rhetoric and arguments to gain followers. Going back in history, where monarchs ruled the throne, there were times that the current leader was considered to be a usurper and they had to gain followers to keep them on the throne. A perfect example would be the house of Windsor and the house of Lancaster who constantly fought for the throne in England.

The art of persuasion was used to keep their followers on their side, and to build armies. Both argued that they were the rightful heir, and that their blood was the one that should be ruling the country. Politics are not that much different during this day and age.

It is such an important skill that it is used in everyday speech to get people on our side for even basic things. When new forms of media are introduced into the world, persuasion is used to challenge why it is better than the old way. For instance, this occurred when the printing press was developed, when newspapers were created, later on when radio and television emerged in society, and today, with the arrival of social media. Each of these mechanisms uses persuasion in a different way to get the point across.

The Six Principles of Persuasion

Persuasion methods are relevant in our current day and age. With different media methods from newspapers, radio, television, billboards, the internet, and social media, companies have to find different ways to reach the general public and sway them to purchase their products or services, listen to their music, read their books, etc. In every advertising, marketing, or communication gimmick, the speaker is trying to convince someone of their point of view.

Even though Aristotle was the first one to document persuasion before the first century, Robert B. Cialdini is the author of modern persuasion. In 1982, he wrote a book called "Influence: The Psychology of Persuasion." The book has been widely known as the pivotal book on marketing. Within this book, Cialdini introduced the world to the 6 principles of Influence.

1. **Reciprocity** – Cialdini's first principle states that people are obligated to give something in return when they receive something. We are wired to return favors and to pay back our debts to them, which essentially means that we want to treat others as they have treated us. This principle leads us to believe that people, by nature, feel obligated to provide favors, discounts, or concessions to those who have done things for them. Psychologically we stress when we feel indebted to other people. For example, you might work for a blog site that offers their readers information that makes their lives better in different areas. All of the information is free when they visit the blog site. However, if your company started selling things on the blog site, your follower based might feel obligated to purchase something because of the free stream of information they have received.

2. **Scarcity** – The principle of scarcity is when people want more of the things they have less of. Cialdini defines this principle as the view of a product becoming more attractive when the availability is limited. People are more influenced to buy something when they feel like the sale is going to run out or the deal will expire soon because they feel like they are going to miss out on something. This is one of the most popular of the principles. Companies use it over and over again to boost sales and earn more money from people. Have you ever driven by a store with a closing sale that has been going on for the past two years? By incorporating a sense of urgency, people are more than likely to come

in and buy something because they might never have the chance again or they won't get it anywhere else.

3. **Authority** – The principle of authority is when people follow the lead of those who are credible and experts in their field. People who have certain job titles and uniforms can pervade their sense of authority into others and lead them to accept what they say without question. This is commonly seen in commercial ads that use doctors to front their campaigns.

4. **Consistency** – The principle of consistency and commitment. It is when people prefer to be consistent with the things they have done or said in life. They have a huge need to be seen by others as consistent because it indicated stability and organization. The need to fulfill the commitment they have promised someone psychologically has to do with their self-image. This can be seen in marketing. For example, marketers might get more visitors on their site to commit to buying something small or free of charge, such as a sample guide or a white paper they can gain when they signup. This increases how the visitor views themselves on the website, and they will eventually start to see themselves as customers and not just visitors. This allows the marketing team to follow up with them and email them offers to buy their products or join their services. It is an easy way to persuade them to become their customer.

5. **Liking** – The principle of liking states that people often prefer to say yes to those they like and say no to those they do not like. Cialdini says that liking someone is meaningful because it adversely affects the chances that you will be influenced by them. This superficial principle can be based on sharing something you like with people, or just based on how attractive you are as a person. For example, all a website has to do is create an awesome About Us page, which gives potential clients information about the company. It is all about having similarities with the people who work for that company. If you have something in

common with them, and/or they are more like you, it is easy for you to find an excuse to buy from them.

6. **Consensus (Social Proof)** – The sixth principle of social proof is when people often look to the actions and behaviors of others to determine what they do, especially when they are uncertain of their own opinions. It's the idea that there is safety in numbers. For example, if you're at work and you see your coworkers working late, you might be more inclined to do the same. If a certain restaurant is constantly busy, you might try it because the more traffic flow that comes in usually means that the food is good. People are often influenced by this principle when they aren't sure of themselves.(Cerejo, 2018).

These six principles have been seen in marketing, advertising, and communication for decades. They are common in businesses and marketing companies that attempt to get the consumer to part with their money. The goal of any business - brick and mortar, internet or app-based - is to make money. You must pay attention to these principles and apply them to your life.

Modern psychology identifies other theories about persuasion, such as:

- Amplification Hypothesis – Certainty hardens attitude when you are talking with someone else, and it can even soften the attitude.
- Bait-and-switch – Great offer that never happens. This happens a lot at car dealerships. The salesman puts a basic car outside at a very low price. Once you take the bait, the salesman trades you up to a model that is more expensive.
- Conversion theory – Minorities can convert the majority of people in instances where the majority does not believe in the cause. However, they continue to go along because it's easier for them and they do not agree with the other option. This is seen a lot when people vote strictly

by a certain party. It is easier to vote for what the party thinks is right without researching to see if their decision is right or not. This can be very dangerous in a lot of cases. It is the idea of the blind leading the blind.

- Door in the Face (DITF) – This occurs when a request is made that is excessive that the person knows that the other person will refuse. This is when they come in with the counteroffer that they know they will accept.
- Foot in the Door (FITD) – This is similar to the Door in the Face option. Except for this time, the person asks for something small and when they receive that, they tend to ask for something bigger, and when that is received, they might ask for something bigger again.
- Forced Compliance – Obligation to obey commands they are coerced in, even if it is against their better judgment.
- Identifiable Victim Effect – Empathizing with one more than many. This works because we can connect with one person much more than a bunch of people we do not know. The individual is humanized and the connection between the two people has now been created.
- Information Manipulation Theory – Breaking one of the four conversational maxims: quantity, quality, relation or manner.
- Persuasion – Factors important in persuasion usually occur when the action or behavior causes someone else to change.
- Priming – Setting up memory to be used later and influences a person's future attitudes, thoughts and behavior.
- Reciprocity Norm – We feel obliged to return favors.
- Scarcity Principle – Making something have limited availability.

- Sleeper Effect – When persuasive messages increase effectiveness over time. Those who use this approach make their message a lot more dramatic than those who delivered it. Once the message becomes important, the source might be forgotten and more credible.
- Social influence – How we are strongly influenced by others.
- Subliminal messages – It is a hidden message in another message that is not noticed or recognized consciously but communicates directly to a person's subconscious.
- Ultimate Terms – Some words are particularly powerful. For instance, God terms can carry a blessing and even demand obedience. Devil terms cause people to feel disgusted. Charismatic terms are associated with things that are observed, like freedom, contribution, etc. Some other powerful words that remind people of their basic needs are safety, control, understanding, greed, health, belonging, esteem, identity, and novelty.
- Weal Ties Theory – How far does influence go? The connection between weak ties such as acquaintances is more important than that of close friends. They can help teach you more things that you might never learn from your friends because they feel or see things the same way that you do.

The study of persuasion has moved from the art of Aristotle's rhetoric, and Cialdini's six principles to a way of life in the modern world. It is imperative that we know all forms of persuasion and how it is being studied in psychology. This is the only way we will be able to defend ourselves against those who try to use this tactic to harm us in one way or another.

Chapter Three: Understanding Dark Persuasion and Covert Persuasion

As stated in the previous chapter, persuasion is a broad term for influence. A speaker can influence a person and their beliefs, attitudes, intentions, motivations, and/or behaviors. And, it is often used for a person's own gain. Immanuel Kant argued that the only moral way that we can even try to manipulate people or their behavior is through rational persuasion. He makes it known that anything else is just immoral and unethical. If this is the case, how can any form of persuasion be anything but rational? How can any part of persuasion be dark if we are given a choice on what to decide?

The difference between persuasion and dark persuasion is the intent. A regular persuader might try to convince their friend to do something without putting much thought into it. They might even be concerned with creating the most good for the most people. This is often true of a diplomat who wants to prevent war between two world powers through creating a political friendship where one had never existed before.

This is not the case with a dark persuader. Their intention is different, they know exactly what they are doing, and they are fully aware of the bigger picture.

One of the things about this type of persuader is that they understand who they are trying to persuade, what their motivation is, and how far they need to go to get what they want. The persuader doesn't contemplate morality in this case because it won't get them what they want. They will find a way to get what they want by any means necessary.

Subliminal messages have been known as the dark art of persuasion for years. People often connect subliminal messages with conspiracy theories against politicians or advertisers and state that the messages are used to manipulate our minds and diminish or change our behaviors. One of the most important things about subliminal messages is that we can never become consciously aware of this type of stimulus, no matter how hard we try. The next thing we need to know is that those who believe in subliminal messages believe that it is a real result of communication that has been deliberately designed to generate a response from people and get them to do things that they wouldn't normally do.

All of this happens on the subconscious level. However, we need to make a distinction between subliminal and supraliminal. Supraliminal is the opposite of subliminal because even though it also evokes responses that consequently influence our behaviors, it can be viewed through the conscious mind.

Freud came up with the term subconscious, which refers to the part of our mind that works on the lower level of our conscious awareness. It is a secret place where we hide our desires, motives and past experiences that we no longer share with our conscious mind. "Our conscious mind gives us executive control of our mind. With our consciousness, we can think, judge, feel and experience with awareness" (Hogan & Speakman, 2013). This is not the case with our subconscious.

Our subconscious is always on autopilot and is more powerful than our regular consciousness when it comes to processing information. This can be dangerous because if someone is using subliminal messages to change how you are thinking or behaving, you are not conscious of what is happening and that can be scary.

What else can they make you do? And how do you stop it?

Covert Persuasion

Covert persuasion is one of the most effective kinds of persuasion and one of the scary things is that the tactics used are completely ethical. They are considered sneaky and underhanded, but they are still ethical. The reason why they are considered dark and dangerous is that they are subtle and seamless, and no one will ever notice that you are even using these tactics. But the tactics will help you convince people to make the choices that you want.

This type of persuasion's goal is to change the mind of your client, audience, etc. without them being aware that their minds are being changed. When their minds are being changed, they will want to purchase your product, try the service you are offering, vote for the candidate you are endorsing, or donate to their idea.

Knowing what words to use is the best way to change your audience's mind. People are often influenced by a smooth talker – hence the art of rhetoric.

There was an experiment that was led by a memory researcher in the 70s that used words to influence participants in the experiment. The participants were shown slides of an accident with a pedestrian and a car, as well as a red Datsun by a yield sign. The participants were asked if they say another car pass the Datsun at the stop sign. However, there was no stop sign in the picture, but there was a yield sign. Once all of the participants heard the question, most of them remembered the stop sign and not the yield sign. When the researcher changed one word in the question, she changed what the participants had seen with their own eyes.

Here are eight steps that explain how to use Covert Persuasion:

1. Identify the source of the problem or situation - This problem is something that you or your company no longer want to experience. It can be high costs, inventory spoilage, ineffective advertising, anything that is not working well within the company that needs to be solved.

2. Help your audience, customers, etc. see that if the problem is not fixed that it will create painful costs on the company. This tactic is highly psychological because it triggers the pain button and makes them feel it before they are aware of how the product, service, or what your company or you can do personally to help.

3. Give your audience the power and ask them what the preferred outcome is. It is important to make sure they choose the best outcome. You can ask, “What would you like to happen?” or “What would be the best result for you?”

4. Next, you want to ask your audience to recognize the positive and negative consequences of their choice. This will help them to accept their decision. You can ask them, “What will this decision do for you?” Their response is forming a new thought direction that will eventually lead them to need what you are offering them.

5. Confirm that the desired result is what they truly want. People often tell others what they think they want to hear. To succeed in persuading them, the audience has to be truthful about what they need, and if making this decision is right for them.

6. This is where you come in. You have to be sure that the result will be good for the audience. It doesn’t help you at all if they agree and then turn around and change their minds. You need to know that they will benefit from all aspects of their decision, which includes what you are offering them.

7. One rule that you need to follow is not to be judgmental about possible negative responses. The audience might have a totally different view

than you, and this is why it is important to know your audience. Take the time to understand and relate to them. Then their responses will become clearer.

8. Another thing to remember is never to tell your audience members that they are wrong. This will put them on the defensive, and they will want to prove that they are right more than listening to what you have to say. It will turn them off with what you are "selling" them.

Remember, covert persuasion is subtle. Most of the time, your audience never catches on and thinks that the decision they are making is what they really want – probably because you skillfully lead them to believe that. The only way that it works is if you can change their minds without them knowing it.

Covert Persuasion and When "No" Means "Yes"

Have you ever rented a car and been adamant that you didn't want insurance, but somehow walked out with it anyway? Have you wondered how they got you to believe that you needed something that you didn't want in the first place? There is a sort of power and control within the resounding no. The rental agent already knows that you are going to walk in telling them what you want and don't want. Most people do not want the extra insurance because they have their own insurance and feel like paying extra for more insurance isn't worth it, especially when you probably aren't going to need it. The resounding "no" is so common that it is something salespeople don't even pay attention to anymore. It is an instant reaction that is driven by the fear of getting swindled into doing something that you do not want. So, you walk in already with your mind made up.

However, the rental agent found a way to get you to buy the product still. Think about it, before they even work on your contract, they go outside and walk you around the cars. During this time, they ask you questions about your trip, what you need it for, and then they start telling you about the amenities of the car – that they carry car seats, and they sell you the coverage based on what appeals to you through the conversation you had. You felt like you had a great conversation with the salesperson, but in reality, they were using the time to prey on you because they know what you will need on this trip you are taking and how what they have to offer will alleviate your stress and/or solve your problem.

When changing your audiences' answer from no to yes, it is about understanding how they make decisions, what appeals to them - by testing the waters – how they remember things, and how they look into the future. Most of the time, people remember important dramatic experiences that turn out badly. The rental agent might ask you if you have car insurance and you tell them that you have what the law requires because you own your car.

This is when they realize that they want to protect their car, but they also want to make you think that they are protecting you from having to pay tons of money out of your pocket. So, they will tell you that they have rental coverage that covers the car bumper to bumper. It is only $11-$14 a day depending on the car size, and there is no deductible. If anything happens to the car, it will be covered, and you will just walk away without paying a dime. This might sound appealing to the customer, but they still feel like they don't need it. So, they tell the rental agent no again.

This is when the agent moves to a story to sway the customer. The agent tells the customer they understand how they feel. Telling them that they buy the coverage doesn't help. They need to tell them a story that they will remember, a dramatic one, which will sway them to their side. The agent brings up an encounter with a previous customer who felt the same way as the current one. The customer was adamant about not getting the coverage that covered the car and rented the car without it.

Another car ended up hitting them in the parking lot, and they walked back in asking if they could get the coverage. The rental agent had to end the rental contract, and not give them the coverage because it is illegal to sell it after the rental agreement has been made and after an accident. The customer ended up paying for the damages out of their pocket, as well as the life of the rental in the shop, which means they had to pay the amount of the rental up to five days. All because they didn't want to pay an extra $30. Due to this story, the current customer ended up purchasing the coverage that covered the car.

When the agent was telling the story to the new customer, all they remembered was the outcome of the crash in the parking lot. They didn't remember anything else about the story, just that they didn't want to go through what the previous customer went through.

Covert Persuasion can be used in different situations, especially when you are trying to win and bring them over to your side. In customer service, you want them to talk about your competitor and discuss their past experiences because if they were satisfied with that experience, they wouldn't be talking to you. One of the things that you have to do is make sure that you don't scare them away so that they do not want to purchase from you.

Have them tell you a story of a great purchase experience they had. This helps you from not scaring them off because you are having them remember a fun experience. For instance, if you are a stockbroker and the potential customer is someone who has lost money in the stock market, you will understand why they don't want to risk money again. But isn't that the risk with the stock market? You're not going to make money every time.

The broker has to be careful in this situation, and they cannot guarantee the potential customer or investor that they will not lose money again. That will be a lie, and that will break their trust right there. The broker has to point out that it is a possibility that they would lose money again. However, it is more likely that they will get typical returns with their investment.

Persuasion research is very clear, especially with covert persuasion. The speaker must show the audience both possible outcomes for them to be successful. If the speaker doesn't indicate that the investor might lose money in the stock market, they will continue to be afraid of it and choose not to invest with your brokerage firm.

When you show them that losing money is a possibility, you also show them what else could happen, within reason. If you make it sound too good to be true, the possible investor will feel like they are being manipulated, and they will still choose not to go with your firm's offer. By keeping it realistic, there is a high chance that they will succumb to your persuasions.

Be clear with your message delivery. If the possible investor lost the first half of the game, they need to come in strong during the second half. Never let what happened in the past determine what they could possibly achieve in the future.

The whole idea of persuading people is to take away their fear of saying yes, which is normal. People tend to have a fear of the unknown and how their life will change. If you are trying to help someone quit smoking, the person will resist at first because the fear of deterring from their normal routine is too much for them. To help them overcome this fear, you will have to substitute their current fear with one that is far worse. Basically, you are scaring them beyond their worst fears. For instance, the speaker tells the person that if they continue to keep smoking every day that it is going to cause you to die. Can you imagine your kids and grandkids standing over your casket? They will remember you the way you looked in that casket. The idea of their family looking over their dead body scares them, especially when it is something that they could have prevented. This is when the speaker makes the fear less painful by helping them cut down. Tell them to start small by cutting down to half a pack a day this month, then only one every day next month and by the next month, you don't need them anymore. Wouldn't it be great to show your family that you don't need to smoke? Wouldn't it be great to show them how healthy you are?

The speaker used fear to persuade the person to stop smoking and then gave them a set of instructions that will help them with the new decision that they made. The person was able to see how changing their life, and going with what you wanted wasn't hard if they worked at it. They weren't going to be worse off because of the decision, but better.

So, once the speaker can change or is persuaded to do what you want them to do, they should be happy that they listened to you and took your advice – whether it be to change their attitude or behavior or purchase what they are selling. This is not always the case, though.

There is a principle known as option attachment. Someone has a choice to purchase one of two puppies. Either puppy would be a good pet to her, but each one is different. They ponder which puppy they could see themselves keeping, and no matter which one they choose, even though they are not aware of it, they worry that the other puppy will be the better of the two because the person did not choose them.

Wouldn't they feel good about the choice they made? You would think that they would be happy, relieved or even comfortable with their decision. Yet, they are miserable. They start to question the decision that they made.

When someone is left thinking about their options too long, they tend to think that whatever they choose, they are losing something by not choosing the other thing. The initial problem is the choice they are left with. The person feels a sense of disappointment and loss when they realize that they have to let the other option go.

Persuasion research indicates that it doesn't matter if the person has personally experienced both options set in front of them, or just imagining one. Whatever option they choose, the other one becomes more attractive because they cannot have it.

The second factor of option attachment is the feeling of loss. The person felt attached to the other option when they were deliberating.

There are two ways to help counteract option attachment:

1. Don't let the person feel any sort of attachment to both of the options. You don't want them to feel a sense of loss. So, make sure that they

don't have a lot of time to make the decision. Tell them that the decision has to be fast.

2. If you have to give them more than one option, make the better option more attractive to them so that they do not spend a lot of time making a decision. Don't let them feel connected with something they are never going to have. Give them info about the option and then make them understand why it is not feasible.

One of the things that the speaker can do is use the option attachment principle to their advantage. If the person is resisting everything that you are doing to persuade them to your side, you can make them feel attached to what you want them to do, making it an easy decision for them. For instance, going back to the puppy scenario from earlier, the person selling the puppies can tell the prospective owner to take one of the puppy's home, and return it if they don't want it. When the person takes the puppy home, they start to get attached and feel a sense of ownership of it. It is hard to give up that feeling without experiencing loss.

Covert persuasion that works starts with the idea that a person's internal beliefs can change when an outside force triggers a transformation. This is where cause and effect work in the scheme of things, i.e., the crash story from earlier. You tell the person that someone else, like your competitor, bought your product and it immensely increased productivity.

Even though the cause and effect arguments are full of holes, statistical arguments tend to confuse people. They want to make an easy decision and not to have to be challenged with thinking. This is why it can be so easy to persuade them if it is done right. People tend to fight for their own beliefs, then switch them. That is why winning an argument makes you feel good.

Some tactics can be used to help persuade people to do what you want:

1. Get the person to write things down. This gets them to participate in the sales process, or the current argument or debate. They could write down important information you are giving them, goals for the coming year, what they want in a car or a house, write information on a stock portfolio or even a timeshare package. The key is to get the person to participate in the process.
2. Build a stronger rapport with your situational audience. If they like you enough as a person, they will probably respond to you positively and buy whatever you are selling them. You can do this by sharing a part of yourself with your audience; this builds trust because they start to think that you became vulnerable in front of them, and continuing to open up to show that you two share some of the same interests increases this type of bond.
3. Synchronize with the audience. If you resemble your audience, in appearance or personality, your voice, breathing, posture, etc. People tend to respond to others that look and act like them. They tend to feel more comfortable. Once you are in sync with your audience, you can take the lead. You will know it is working when the other person is mimicking you, as well.
4. Get the audience to move around if your persuasion attempt is not working. It has been proven that motion can bring forth emotion. You can either stand up, walk around the room, take the person out to lunch or coffee. Changing the location and physical position can help change the state of their mind.
5. Induce reciprocity. Building rapport helps you build a foundation of concern, compassion, caring interest, and a desire for your audience's wellbeing is an important way to make them feel like they are building a strong bond with you. When you pace and lead your audience, the process creates a sense of comfort for both of you because you are

moving along at their pace. After the rapport is built, you can move on to your presentation.

After using these tactics, it is important to use the right words, questions, and stories to deliver the message you want to tell your subject. Some powerful words that you can use are you, money, save, results, health, easy, love, discovery, proven, new, safety, and guarantee. Ask them questions that help keep you in control of the thought processes of the audience. You have to remember that the other person won't be conscious of your persuasion techniques. They will feel like they are in control of the decisions they make, even if you lead them to the decisions. Once they make these decisions, they become committed to them because they are their choice. This is very important in the art of persuasion. The speaker never wants to just win the sale; they want to win the audience for life (Hogan & Speakman, 2013).

Chapter Four: Common Situations of Persuasion

As was stated in the previous chapters, when a person understands how their mind works, they can protect themselves against those who would persuade them and do them harm.

We have all been victims of a sleazy salesperson, either at a car dealership, on the phone, to someone we met in a store. These people will do whatever they can to get us to buy what they are selling, even if we didn't need or want it. Think about walking into a jewelry store. Now think about walking into a jewelry store, and your goal is to buy an engagement ring. You're aware that you are going to drop some money on an item, but you have a budget and you aren't going over it. You walk in the store with your friend, who promises you that they know a lot about jewelry, their uncle is a jeweler. However, when you walk inside the store, you notice that everything is overpriced and way out of your budget. Even the cheapest rings were more than you wanted to spend. You talk to the salesman, and they tell you that the price of the rings has gone up because of inflation. This is the best time to buy right now. Everyone is proposing. And he tells you that the more expensive the ring is, the better it is. Who wants to buy a cheap ring for their future wife? You are not only investing in a symbol of your love, but you are investing in your future.

This scenario is important because it shows that certain behaviors trigger behaviors in humans. This is known as the trigger feature. The prices of the rings became a trigger for quality. The rings were priced more than they were worth, but the salesman made it seem like the more they were, the better the quality. His customer ended up spending the money because he wanted to invest in his future, and he didn't want his future wife to think he was cheap.

To overcome the manipulation from people like the jeweler, we need to understand how the principles work. The contrast principle of perception states that if we pick up a box that is light and then a heavy one. We will automatically think that the heavy box is heavier by contrast. In the scenario above, the jeweler would show the customer a more expensive ring before a less expensive one to get him to buy something for his future wife. It is a tactic to ensure the jeweler makes a sale no matter what (Cy, 2018).

Building Anticipation

We are all familiar with this tactic. Recently everyone has been talking about the end of Game of Thrones and how they were disappointed. Every season, when we watch our favorite shows, butts glued to the couch, eyes to the screen, we are in anticipation of what is going to happen before, during, and after the commercial break, the next episode and the climax at the end of the season. Sometimes we are left waiting, and sometimes we are left disappointed. However, we become hooked based on the anticipation of what is going to happen next. This is known as the power of the *open loop*.

The open loop is a powerful way to direct focus and build a type of desire or anticipation. The persuader has now grabbed the attention of their subject and can build a bigger rapport with them. They have them wrapped around their finger, waiting to do their bidding.

What can I do to make sure that I don't fall into people's traps?

People that try to persuade you are going to try to figure out things about you that will make it easier for them to get you to make the choice that they want.

First, you need to pay attention to them and how they are viewing you. One of the ways that you can protect yourself is noticing if they are copying your body language. People find that their subjects are easier to persuade if they are more comfortable with them. Like-minded people have the same body language make you feel more comfortable and a little bit more susceptible.

If these people are mimicking the way that you are holding your hands and sitting the same way as you, change your movements and see if they continue to mimic you. If you notice this occurring, this is a good time to call them out on it.

Make sure that you pay attention to what you are focusing on, and not just on what they are focusing on. Do not zone out or start to daydream because they want to try to lead you unconsciously to do something that you don't want to do. If they notice that you are not directly paying attention to them, they will use this to their advantage to manipulate you in a way that works for them.

This is why you have to make sure that you don't take everything they say at face value and read between the lines. Those who are well versed in persuasion tactics will often use language that has hidden meanings. For example, "Diet, nutrition, and sleep with me are the most important things, don't you think" (Louv, 2014). What is the underlying meaning of the question? If you weren't focusing, you might agree with this sentence because all three of those things are important to you as well. However, listen to how the sentence was said, "Diet, nutrition and sleep with me are the most important things." The sentence should say that diet, nutrition, and sleep are most important to me. But the reason the person said what he said was that he wanted the subject to sleep with him... that is why sleep with me was subtly put into the middle of the sentence because the subject was not fully focused on everything that was being said, and they agreed to something they were not consciously aware of.

Don't agree to anything. This is important because, throughout the whole conversation, the person who is trying to persuade you to do something is trying to build a rapport with you, so they can figure out how to get you to do what they want. They will continue to try to get you to make a fast decision on something. But, if you feel like they are steering the conversation in a certain direction, leave. Come back in 24 hours before you decide to make any decision. Remember, this is your choice.

Another thing to remember is not to make any rash or emotional decisions because you might regret them later. These people know how to use persuasion techniques to get you to do things on impulse. If you feel like you are not thinking rationally, then come back when you are, or not at all.

The last thing that you can do to protect yourself is to trust your gut. If you feel like something isn't right, it probably isn't, and you definitely should listen to that. Those who are trying to swindle you usually give off a weird vibe in and a feeling in the pit of your stomach. If you are bold enough, you can either leave or tell them to respect you enough to come at you without trying to swindle you. They either will or they won't. But if they are skilled in their tactics, they are going to deny what they did to get you to believe that they were genuine with you.

Hopefully, these tactics will be helpful when trying to protect yourself against dark and covert persuaders.

Chapter Five: Understanding Dark Manipulation

Attila the Hun is a well-known name in history and is viewed as a barbaric ruler. Coming from a land of nomads, he became their leader and learned to be as ruthless as the hostile empires that surrounded him. He ruled over the Hunnic empire and had a sense of control over Germany, Poland, parts of Russia and Hungary. He set a goal, pummeled through Europe and Asia, and almost conquered the Empire of Rome. Attila was determined to make a way for himself in the world. He and his armies moved across Europe and Asia, pushing across the borders and harassing the Romans. Most of the battles set against the Romans left the Romans badly defeated, and they paid large sums of gold in tribute to Attila and his empire, which was slowly conquering theirs. The only way that he was defeated was through a combination of armies from Rome and the Visigoths. This was the only way to stop his destruction and to keep control of their lands.

This man was a great general who accomplished great things. However, he was also a narcissist. He was known for his temper and his rages. He was often jealous, had a huge ego, and lacked empathy. He knew what he wanted and went out and took it, no matter the risk or the cost. Attila the Hun was often known as the Scourge of God, and the destruction and wake that he left behind were what made other people fear him, which caused them to do their bidding. Such as the Roman Empire when they payed him tithes.

Dark Manipulation, otherwise known as psychological manipulation, is a form of social influence that aims to change how someone behaves or perceives others through indirect, deceptive, and/or underhanded tactics. The manipulator uses these tactics to advance their own interests at another's expense. The methods that they use can be viewed as devious and exploitative.

Now, social influence is not always dark and negative. It depends on the manipulator's agenda and how they use their tactics.

What kind of outcome do they want to have? For instance, people have often used interventions, with emotional manipulation, to help their loved ones change from their bad habits or behaviors. When social influence is harmless, the person has a right to choose what they are being offered or reject it. They are not forced into making a certain decision. If this is not the case, then it is dark manipulation, and the person is using their interests as an advantage to gain something from the other person.

Some of the things that motivate manipulators are:

1. The need to feel in control due to a feeling of powerlessness in their lives.
2. The need to feel a sense of power or authority over others and to lift their self-esteem.
3. The need to fulfill a sense of boredom. Often manipulators consider hurting others as a type of game.
4. Sometimes the manipulator is not consciously aware of what they are doing. They often feel like their own emotions are invalid, and they

forecast those emotions onto others, i.e., trying to justify their fear of commitment.

5. Having a hidden agenda that can be criminal. This can include financial manipulation that is often used on the elderly or unprotected wealthy who have been often targeted to obtain their financial assets.

George K. Simon, a psychologist and author, states that the role of the manipulator plays a huge role in being successful in the art of dark manipulation. There are three things that the manipulator must be aware of and know:

1. How to conceal their aggressive intentions and behaviors and how to be sweet and pleasant to get what you want, i.e., buttering someone up.
2. Know their victims' vulnerabilities. This will allow the manipulator to know what tactics would be more effective.
3. Having no moral qualms about being ruthless, as well as not caring if you hurt the victim in some way. The end is justifying the means, as the saying goes.

The Dark Triad

Personality Vulnerabilities

Manipulation predators or dark manipulators use many techniques to control their victims. They look for a certain types of people with certain types of personalities. Those types of personalities that are often prey to manipulators are those with low or no self-esteem, those who are easy to please, those with low or no self-confidence, who have no sense of assertiveness and are very naïve.

Let's explain these personality traits in more detail:

- Those who are naïve find it virtually impossible to accept the fact that particular people in their lives can be cunning, devious, and ruthless. They will constantly deny that they are being victimized.
- Those who are over-conscientious give the manipulator the benefit of the doubt, even if they know in the back of their mind, they are right. They are hoping they are not and take the blame.
- Those who have low self-confidence start to doubt themselves and what they are experiencing, they are not assertive and they easily defensive because they don't want to make waves.
- Those who are emotionally dependent have a submissive and dependent personality. When the victim is more emotionally dependent, the manipulator has an easier time exploiting and manipulating them.
- Those who over-intellectualize want to believe the manipulator and try to understand their reason for harming others, especially the victim themselves.

Those who tend to use others to their own advantage fall under the "Dark Triad'. As defined earlier in this book, it is "a set of traits that include the tendency to seek admiration and special treatment (otherwise known as narcissism), to be callous and insensitive (psychopathy) and to manipulate others (Machiavellianism" (Whitbourne, 2013). Studies have indicated that the triad consists of a lot of undesirable behaviors, such as aggressiveness, impulsivity, and sexual opportunism.

When people show signs of these characteristics, they are trying to get away with using others to get what they want. Each one of these personality traits can make life difficult for people, but all of these traits combined can be dangerous to anyone's mental health. Those who have any one of these personality traits show some of these behaviors: seeking out multiple sex partners, acting out aggressively to get what they want, having high or low self-esteem, and not viewing themselves highly. Most of these traits are shown by men (Whitbourne, 2013).

Knowing more about the dark triad will help you protect yourself from those who wish to manipulate you and use you to their advantage. Research has been done to analyze the differences between all three personality traits within the triad. They have found that all three malevolent personalities "act aggressively out of self-interest and lack empathy and remorse. They're skilled at manipulation and exploit and deceive others, though their motivations and tactics vary. They violate social norms and moral values and lie, deceive, cheat, steal, and bully. It's thought that genetic factors underlie their personality to some degree" (Lancer, 2018).

However, psychopathy and Machiavellianism are more related because of their malicious behavior. Those who fall under the narcissist umbrella are very defensive and are surprisingly fragile. Their arrogance and ego are just a cover for their feelings of inadequacy. Men are prone to psychopathic traits and behavior due to biological factors (testosterone), as well as social norms.

It is important to note that people who have one of these three personality disorders are not trustworthy, are selfish, are not straightforward, are not kind, or modest, and they do not comply or compromise; which are all qualities that are not good for any type of relationship. If you know someone that exuberates any of the dark triad traits, you might want to see if you are a victim of any of these techniques.

Manipulation Techniques

Lying is one of the very first techniques that manipulators use. It is a technique that pathological liars or psychopaths use when they want to confuse their victims. If they are constantly lying to them, their victims will often be unaware of the truth. Those who use this tactic have no moral or ethical apprehension about it.

Telling half-truths or only telling part of a story is another tactic that can be used to manipulate someone. People like this will often keep things to themselves because it puts the victim at a disadvantage. They can get what they want by waiting to tell them the rest of the story until their needs are met.

Being around someone who has frequent mood swings can often make a person vulnerable to their manipulations. Not knowing what mood that person will be in, whether they will be happy, sad, or angry can be a very useful tactic for the manipulator. It keeps the victim off balance and easy to manipulate because they will often do what the manipulator wants to keep them in a good mood.

Another tactic that is often used by narcissists is known as love bombing. This doesn't necessarily mean that you have to be in a relationship but can be used in a friendship as well. Those that use this tactic will charm the victim to death and have them believe that this is the best relationship or friendship that has ever happened to them. They will use the victim for what they want, and then when they are done, they drop them and the victim has no idea what happened.

A tactic that can be used in extreme cases by the manipulator is that of punishment. This makes the victim feel guilty for something they did wrong, even if they didn't do anything at all. Some of the punishments that they can inflict on their victims are consistent nagging, shouting, mental abuse, giving them the silent treatment, and even as bad as physical violence.

Denial is often a tactic that is used when a manipulator feels pushed in a corner, and they feel like they will be exposed for the fake that they are. In this instance, they will manipulate the victim into believing that they are doing the very thing the manipulator is being accused of.

Spinning the truth is a tactic often used by politicians. It is used to twist the facts to suit their needs or wants. Sociopaths use this technique to disguise their bad behavior and justify it to their victims.

Minimizing is when a manipulator will play down their behavior and/or actions. They move the blame onto the victim for overreacting when their actions are harmful, and the person has a valid reason for feeling the way they do.

It is often interesting when the manipulator pretends to become the victim. They do this to gain sympathy or compassion from their real victims. They do this so that their victims feel a sense of responsibility to help and end their suffering, especially if they feel that they are the cause of that person's suffering.

Another way that the manipulator can move the blame onto the victim is by targeting the victim and accusing them of wrongdoing. The victim will then start to defend themselves, while the manipulator hides their manipulation away from the victim. This can be dangerous because the victim is so focused on defending themselves that they forget to notice what is right in front of them.

Using the positive reinforcement tactic tricks the victim into thinking that they are getting something for helping the manipulator get what they want. This can be through purchasing them expensive presents, praising them, giving them money, constantly apologizing for their behavior, giving them lots of attention and all-around buttering them up.

There are times when a person knows where they stand with someone. However, in any type of relationship, the manipulator might keep moving the goal just to confuse their victim because they thought that everyone was still on the same page.

Another manipulation tactic that manipulators like to use is known as diversion. This tactic is commonly used to divert a certain conversation away from what the manipulator is doing. The new topic is created to get the victim to lose focus on what the manipulator is doing or trying to do.

Sarcasm is a tactic that can be used to lower the self-esteem and confidence of a victim through embarrassment. The manipulator will use sarcasm – usually saying something about the victim- in front of other people. This gives the manipulator power over the victim because they just made them feel very small.

Guilt trips are another tactic that a manipulator will use against their victim. In this instance, they will often tell their victims that they don't care about them or love them; they will indicate that they are selfish and that their life is easy. It keeps the victim confused and anxious because they want to please the manipulator by letting them know that they care about them and will do anything for them.

Using flattery is the exact opposite of guilt-tripping. In this instance, the manipulator will use charm, praise or other types of flattery to gain the victim's trust. They victim enjoys the compliments and lets their guard down.

Another way that a manipulator will move the blame is to play the innocent card when the victim accuses them of their tactics. They will act shocked or show confusion at the accusation. The act of being surprised is convincing to the victim, and it makes them question their judgment and if what they are feeling is wrong.

A dangerous tactic that a manipulator can use is that of extreme aggression. Rage and aggression are used to force the victim to submit. The anger and rage are a tactic that scares the victim to stop talking about the conversation. They pretty much want to help keep the manipulator's anger in check.

Isolation is another dangerous tactic used by manipulators. It is a control mechanism that is used by manipulators to keep their victims from their family, friends, and loved ones who can expose the manipulator for who they really are. The manipulator might know that their victim can be manipulated, but their friends and family can see right through them, and they are not done using their victim yet.

And, one of the last tactics that manipulators, such as psychopaths and sociopaths use is that of fake love and empathy. These types of people do not know how to love others besides themselves and have a hard time loving others and showing empathy towards others. They use this tactic to entangle themselves into their victims' lives to extract what they want from them (Learning Mind, 2012).

Remember that Dark Manipulation is a very dangerous thing and not something that anyone would want to be caught up in if they can help it. Therefore, it is important to read this chapter to protect yourself against anyone who would try to take advantage of you and manipulate you to get what they want. The more knowledge you have about these devious acts, the easier it is to protect yourself from it.

Chapter Six: What is Covert Manipulation?

In the previous chapter, we discussed dark manipulation in detail. However, for comparison reasons dark manipulation otherwise known as psychological manipulation, is a form of social influence that aims to change how someone behaves or perceives others through indirect, deceptive, or underhanded tactics. The manipulator uses these tactics to advance their interests at another's expense. The methods that they use can be viewed as devious and exploitative.

Covert manipulation is emotional manipulation that "occurs when a person who wants to gain power and control over you uses deceptive and underhanded tactics to change your thinking, behavior, and perceptions" (Psychopaths and Love, 2013). This type of manipulation functions below your conscious awareness. One of the scary things about it is that it holds you mentally enslaved. Those who fall victim to covert manipulation don't always realize what's happening while it is happening, and that is the scary part. Those who are skilled at covert manipulation find ways to convince you to put your self-confidence, sense of self-worth and your emotional well-being into their hands. Once you give them that sort of power over you, they will continuously chip away at your self-esteem and destroy your identity until you have nothing left.

Two types from the Dark Triad: psychopaths and narcissists, manipulate in mostly the same way, but psychopaths are considered to be the most dangerous of the manipulators. Here are some reasons why they are considered to be one of the most dangerous:

- They see themselves as superior to others.
- They view others as prey. They hunt their prey to satisfy their needs.
- Psychopaths do not have the capacity to love
- Psychopaths lack empathy
- Psychopaths have no guilt or remorse, as well as no conscience
- They think that life is a game where they take power and exert control over their victims to get what they want: possibly sex, money, or influence, and then destroy them emotionally, physically, spiritually, and mentally in the process.
- All of the things psychopaths do because they want to satisfy their needs in any way they can. Once they get bored or start to hate you – when they have won - they leave and move on to someone else.

It is important to note that covert manipulators cannot have a real relationship because they do not know how. Most of them have had a plan set up since the day they met their victims. They have skills in reading their victims and learning their weaknesses, strengths, fears, even their dreams and desires. They want to look like they are invested in their victims and will even use all that they learn, or their victim divulges to them against them with a list of manipulation techniques that they have personally chosen for their victim. Manipulators have a hunger for control, authority, and power, and they will do whatever it takes to feel like they are in control of their victim and take everything they can get from them, even if it means harming harm.

Psychopaths are overtly charming because that is how they reel their victims in. They do this to make their victims feel comfortable like they won the jackpot. For instance, if they just got into a relationship with their victim, they will play the part of the loving boyfriend or girlfriend, winning them over, making them feel magical and excited. They will make the victim fall in love, acting like they are the person their victim has been waiting for their whole lives, and then they pull the rug out from under them. They are very talented and know how to hide their personalities and their plans, which is to get you to believe that they are in love with you and that they will do everything they can to make you happy and to continue to believe in the romance of the relationship in to hook the victim and prey on their vulnerabilities that will lead to abuse.

Once they have hooked the victim, the whole purpose of the relationship will move from loving to demeaning, humiliating, misusing, confusing, and lowering their self-confidence, respect, self-worth, and self-esteem. They will bring out the fake person that the person fell in love with, to keep their victims in the relationship, guilt trip them into believing that they are the best thing in their lives, and will die if they lose them. This is why the victim will do whatever it takes to save their relationship from destruction.

The victim starts to accept any type of affection when it is given, which is hardly at all. They won't talk about what they want or need in the relationship anymore, what they feel, or what their fears are. They might feel like they can't confide in their partner anymore, but the manipulator doesn't care because they never did in the first place. They view those things as weaknesses and will start making the victim turn around and blame themselves for things going wrong. The victim will start overthinking everything that is said in a conversation, breaking apart every word and mood, and will start to become confused about what was happening. Everything in the victim's life will start to suffer: their personal life, their job, their other relationships, and their physical and mental health will suffer.

The manipulator will continue to keep their victim around until they are a desperate mess - one they turned their victim into. At this point, they will end up becoming bored with their victims and will end up leaving them, and the victim must try to pick up the pieces of themselves.

While the manipulator has left to find their next victim, the previous victim will "struggle with feelings of confusion and severe emotional pain. Many also experience obsessive thoughts, rage, lost self-esteem, insomnia, anxiety, panic, fear, an inability to trust, use of alcohol or drugs, lack of support, and physical illness. Irrational and sometimes extreme behavior can occur, such as isolation and withdrawal from friends, family and society, and suicidal thoughts or actions" (Psychopaths & Love, 2013).

These manipulators never wanted love because they are incapable of it, as we stated earlier. Even if they had a sense of attraction to their victim – in any form- it was just to use them because it would make it easier for them to like the victim in some way. How else could they spend all that time with them?

The most important thing to remember about these types of people is that they have a disorder, and even though it doesn't make it right, it does show the victim that there is nothing wrong with them. We all have fallen victim to manipulations once in our lives, even when we are strong-minded. These people know how to find what makes others vulnerable and then do what they can to hook their victims into thinking they are amazing people. They can do this for many reasons; maybe they have insecurities about themselves that they cannot face. So, they project those insecurities on their victims. It might be a survival mechanism because they never had what they think they desire, and they have no other way of knowing how to get it.

Those who have fallen victim to these manipulations are not alone in their suffering and should find support groups or individual therapy to help put their lives back together and move on. They will be happier for it because they might recognize some of the techniques, so they do not fall prey to them again.

Chapter Seven: Common Situations of Manipulation

Emotional intelligence is defined as "a person's ability to recognize and understand emotions and use that information to guide decision making" (Bariso, 2018). This particular skill can be taught, enhanced, and sharpened. Some people use and abuse their skills in emotional intelligence as a dark manipulation tactic to control their victims.

Here is a list of things that a manipulator will do and what you can do to protect yourself:

1. They prey on their victim's fears – They will magnify and stress certain points to scare their victim into action.

a. This is why it is important to watch out for statements that make you into a coward or afraid that you are going to miss out on something. Know all of the facts before you make any decisions.

2. Manipulators use the art of deception to harm their victims. Of course, they do not want to give you all of the information upfront because then you might catch on to what they are planning to do or are already doing. They will hide the whole truth or only give one side of the story.

a. This is why it is important not to believe everything that you hear. Question things, especially if they sound fishy. Look for credible sources to get all the facts.

3. Your happiness becomes the manipulator's advantage. Have you ever made a decision when you were in a great mood? Was it easier for you to say yes, and to grab an amazing opportunity that you wouldn't have considered before? This is normal. Those who manipulate know how to use this great mood to their advantage.

a. Make sure that you start becoming aware of your moods, positive and negative. This way, when you are making decisions, you can make a more balanced one.

4. A favor for a favor is what manipulators do best. They are aware that if they do you a favor – even if it is small – then you will do something for them.

a. We all know that it feels good to give more than to receive. However, it is good to know your limits and not to be afraid to say no if you have too.

5. They feel more comfortable in a place where they can be more dominant. This is why they might want to hang out in a space like their home, office, or some other place they are familiar with.

a. This is why it is important to meet in a space that is public and neutral. If you do end up going somewhere that is comfortable for them, ask for a drink and get to know them until you start feeling comfortable.

6. Sometimes manipulators will start asking a lot of questions. So, instead of talking about themselves, they will ask their victims questions that will showcase their weaknesses to find out information that they can use to their advantage.

a. Be alert when people want to know all about you but don't reveal any information about themselves.

7. They talk fast. A lot of times, manipulators will talk fast, so you don't catch what they are saying, or they will speak in phrases or use big words that give them an advantage over their victims.

a. If you do not understand what they are saying, it is okay to ask them to clarify what they said. Repeat their point back to them and ask for examples if needed. Regaining control of the conversation is a way that you can determine if what you are doing is right or wrong.

8. They are emotionally negative through raising their voice or having aggressive body language to indicate that they are upset. They do this because they want to manipulate their victims to change their behavior.

a. Do not react right away. Take a moment to consider and take a walk if needed.

9. The manipulator only gives their victims a small window to act on the decision they want you to make. This is their way of trying to force you to decide before you can think about it rationally.

a. Do not make any rash decisions, especially without all of the information. If they will not give you the time you need to make the right decision, then don't make a decision at all..

10. They will often ignore you. This can be through calls, texts, emails and other ways of communication. By making you wait for them, they feel like they have the upper hand because now they are placing a sense of doubt and insecurity in your mind about the relationship.

a. If you keep contacting the person and they don't respond, you can either wait for them to respond or you can give them a deadline when they have to respond to you. If it persists, maybe you need to look elsewhere for someone who will give you the attention that you deserve (Bariso, 2013).

If you study and use these strategies when you feel like someone is manipulating you, you will protect yourself from a world of hurt.

Chapter Eight: What is Deception?

Martin was a very successful businessman, a loving husband and father, and a model example in the community. No one would have guessed that he led a double life. Martin had married Samantha 10 years ago and they had three kids together. They had a house in upstate New York, and they were very active in their community. Martin's practice took him to the city a couple of times a week, and this is where he met Amber. They had been seeing each other for over three years, and they had a set of twins the previous year. They had purchased an apartment on the Upper East Side, and they had a great life together. Martin managed to keep a schedule of seeing both women and being a part of both families for three years. It wouldn't be until their children grew older and found their father's different social media pages, did his two lives become public to his two wives. Both women confronted each other and ended up coming to terms. They confronted Martin together and kicked him out of both of their houses for deceiving them.

Deception is a big or small act that can either be kind or cruel. It is the act itself that causes someone to believe that it is untrue. Like Mary and Amber did with Martin. They had no idea that he was cheating on them and had another family on the other side of the state. They would have never known unless it was revealed to them by their kids.

Deception isn't always a bad thing. Even honest, trustworthy people can be deceiving. Studies have shown that the average person tells several lies a day. Some of these lies can be big, and some are lies of omission or even white lies. People don't always lie to cover up something big and bad. A lot of times it is because they don't want to hurt anyone's feelings.

Deception does not always happen externally either. People have found ways to even lie to themselves. This can be due to maintaining healthy self-esteem or keeping up with serious illusions that are out of their control. Not all self-deception is harmful. For instance, telling yourself that you can accomplish a goal that you are working on results in a positive outcome.

However, most of the time, deception is harmful and dangerous.

Let's face it; no one likes to be deceived or lied too. Look at how the world reacted with the Bill Clinton and Monica Lewinski scandal. They wanted to impeach him for lying to United States citizens.

The truth is, everyone lies. There are many reasons why they do it. For instance, Psychology Today wrote that "some experts suggest that a certain amount of deception may be necessary for maintaining a healthy, functioning society" (PsychologyToday.com, 2018).

We have to face the fact that they are going to be people who will attempt to mislead us by intentionally withholding information that we might need to know.

If you are afraid of misleading others, you can ask yourself why you are not telling the complete truth if you have nothing to hide?

The fact that deception is so broad makes it difficult to acknowledge and see by the person doing the deceiving. When the term is broken down, i.e., a blatant lie, it makes the person feel a little less guilt and they don't have to be held accountable for their behavior. It helps them think that they didn't do anything wrong. Narrowing down the term makes the person feel better about themselves and they can continue to mislead, omit the truth, or lie to others. It is easier to be deceptive when you don't think that you are doing something wrong. This lack of morality can be harmful, not only to the victim but to yourself as well.

This is why people avoid telling an obvious lie when they know that someone can find out the facts or already know some of the facts. This is a very risky and bold move. Most of the time, people will tell a bold lie when they know that their story is not verifiable, and the person will take what they say at face value. This is why people are more comfortable telling lies of omission when they can. These lies make them feel less guilty because they are telling the truth, minus a few details. It is important to note that those who are being lied to don't see this lie as any different from the old one. They still feel like they are being lied too.

Researchers Jeremy Yip and Wharton Maurice Schweitzer have defined the link between anger and deceiving others. It is a common practice within organizations, especially during job interviews and even in negotiations. People often make things up about themselves on their resumes and even in their interviews because they want to make a positive first impression to get the job.

They found that incidental anger, which is anger that can be triggered by anything, leads to deception. When people get angry, they are more likely to lie than when they aren't angry. They aren't thinking about their actions anymore and how that impacts others because they are trying to make themselves look better. Anger makes the person less empathetic, and they could care less about them in general. They are more focused on themselves, which is known as self-serving deception. "These are lies that advantage the liar at the expense of a target. When people are telling self-serving lies, they're often engaging in this calculus between what are the costs and benefits for themselves, but also what are the costs and benefits for others. What we find is that anger influences these calculations, where angry people become more focused on the benefits to themselves and discount the harm that they may cause others. This leads them to engage in deception" (Wharton.upenn.edu, 2017).

New research shows that children as young as two develop tendencies to lie. Lying is considered a developmental milestone that is put in the same category as crawling and walking because those who lie have to plan, pay attention to detail, and can see the situation like the people they are trying to manipulate.

It is true that lying does not come naturally and that most of us have to work at it unless there are incentives. For instance, if there is money involved, people often choose to be dishonest. This indicates that lying has to do with people's inability to resist temptation. Lying becomes easier when we can rationalize it, when we are stressed, tired, and when we are seeing others who are being dishonest. The only thing that keeps us from lying is when there are others around who morally disapprove of it, and they are watching us.

"Manipulative deceptions occur when deceivers hide, omit, distort, and exaggerate information to control your choices and decisions. These deceptions are the tools of con artists, politicians, unscrupulous marketers, propagandists, False New reporters, and nearly everyone else who seeks advantage at your expense" (Knaus, 2011).

Mendacious deceptions are acts that can cause major harm and stress. They are immoral acts where the liar doesn't use their conscience. The person who is trying to deceive will blame others for what they are doing to lead the focus somewhere else.

Evil deceptions are meant to cause deadly and malicious harm to their victims. These people deliver their plans though tyrannical actions. "They are masters of paradoxical defenses, but here they also use positive labels, such as the society of democratic actions, to conceal opposite intentions" (Knaus, 2011).

One of the ways that you can protect yourself against manipulative, mendacious and evil deception is through enlightened skepticism. This skill is a way to find out the truth about what someone is telling you through fact-finding and asking questions. This is a beneficial skill because it helps a person work on their critical thinking, helps teach them who they can and cannot trust, and helps them figure out who is trying to take advantage of them.

Here are a few questions that can be asked in help get closer to the truth when you are trying to avoid being deceived:

- Is any part of the person's statement truthful?
- Is their statement consistent with what goes on in the real world?
- Is it verifiable?
- Do I gain anything from accepting and acting on their statement?
- Do I lose anything from accepting and acting on their statement?
- What do they gain if you buy into their statement?
- Is there any information that is exaggerated or downplayed during the statement?
- Is the idea too good to be true?
- Would you advise anyone to accept the validity of the statement without question?
- Is anything in the statement being said forcefully?

When you ask yourself these questions, you will notice that you are being fooled less often. Those who try and deceive you will soon learn that you can see past their lies and they will move onto easier targets. Another way that you can practice your skills at detecting deception is through observation. This can be done while watching opinion shows on television. Make sure you pay close attention to the talking points because you will see examples of omissions, half-truths, bold lies, overgeneralization, hyperbole, as well as emotional reasoning that controls reasoning and narrative to shape public opinion on the show.

Another way you can observe deception behavior is through watching commercials. This will help you with your critical thinking skills by finding lies, types of exaggerations, and even omissions. If you find some gaps in the information that you are viewing, it might be better to wait to make a critical judgment until you know more.

Since pride can be one of the major factors of being deceived, admitting that you are wrong can be a way to protect yourself against deceivers. "Benjamin Franklin writes of his decision to start admitting that he could be wrong when he put forth arguments. He said that by doing that, and by hearing people out when he disagreed with them rather than jumping in with his own point of view, he reduced his fear of being wrong" (Snow, 2016). The willingness to admit that you are wrong and to completely change your mind can save you from being fooled into deception.

Just like manipulation and persuasion, the best way to protect yourself against those who would harm you is knowledge. Knowing more about these personality traits gives you a leg up on the people who are trying to take advantage of you. However, knowing all of the different ways that people can use you and the lengths that they will go will help you become better at detecting when you might be part of a harmful situation. So, continue to study the techniques that were provided in the beginning of this book, and get familiar with them. You will be glad that you did when you get yourself out of some sticky spots time and time again.

Chapter Nine: The Power of Hypnosis

In 1899 there was a case of an Austrian woman who had major stomach problems. She couldn't keep her food down, no matter how hard she tried. And, she tried everything. A group of doctors decided to try hypnosis on the woman to see if it would help. At first, the doctors suggested - under hypnosis – that she could eat, but that she would keep her food down this time. Without prevail, she started vomiting the moment that she ate. They kept repeating the suggestion, and it didn't work. No matter how many times they had tried.

After much deliberation, one of the doctors came up with a suggestion that might work. He thought that instead of telling her stomach to keep the food down, he trick her mind into believing that she hadn't eaten anything at all. This way, if there was nothing in her body, how could she throw it up? The woman ate a full meal, and just as quick as she was done, she forgot that she had eaten at all. The suggestion was repeated a few times while putting her under hypnosis and she was able to start keeping her food down (Yetter, 2017).

People have been skeptical of hypnosis since its inception. They have questioned its validity and often attribute it to a farce, or something you see magicians do at events. Unless you have experienced it personally, you wouldn't even consider it to be something you would try. This might be because you don't know much about it and haven't conducted any research. This is where this chapter of the book comes in.

History of Hypnosis

Hypnosis was "coined in the early 19th century by Etienne Felix d'Henin de Cuvillers, a Frenchman interested in the role of suggestion on the mind, and the mental and behavioral processes that took place when someone fell into a hypnotic trance" (Cohut, 2017). There is a huge debate on whether de Cuvillers came up with the term, or if it was Dr. James Braid, a Scottish Surgeon. Whatever the case, the idea of hypnosis was born in the 18th century. Franz Mesmer, a German doctor, held claim to something called animal magnetism. Animal magnetism is a fluid that can flow between people, animals, plants, and other things. This invisible fluid can be used to manipulate or influence other people's actions and behaviors.

Of course, he was considered to be a quack, and his practices were laughed about by many. But, the idea of being able to influence people's behavior and actions became a topic of interest in the medical field. Through persistence in the 20th and 21st centuries, the art itself has continued to be researched and studied. Hypnotic specialists have given the art a name for itself through better understanding. People are more aware of what it can do and how it can be used for health reasons.

What Exactly is Hypnosis and How Does it Work?

Hypnosis is defined as "a kind of top-down regulation of conscious awareness, a process in which 'mental representations' override physiology, perception, and behavior" (Cohut, 2017).

Hypnosis consists of two parts: Induction and Suggestion.

1. Induction is the first suggestion that is offered during the hypnotic process.
2. Hypnotic suggestion is the mind's capability to experience the suggested changes in their body, emotions, thoughts, and behaviors. The suggestion part of the actual hypnosis is what changes the person's actions or behaviors. The suggestions are more than implied; they provoke the person to react involuntarily. The person doesn't have any control over the suggestion itself.

As we have read in other chapters in the book, some people are more susceptible to suggestive influence than others. Those who are more susceptible to influence are more than likely to be more controlled while hypnotized.

"Neuroimaging techniques have shown that highly suggestible people exhibit higher activity levels in the prefrontal cortex, anterior cingulate cortex, and parietal networks of the brain during phases of hypnosis" (Cohut, 2017). These areas within the brain deal with functions related to memory and perception, processing emotions and task learning.

So, how does hypnosis work? Scientists are still unclear about it. However, they are working on finding out more about it and how it affects our mind. But until then, this is what we have come up with.

Medically, and therapeutically, hypnosis is a treatment option that helps people cope with different medical conditions. It is often conducted by a hypnotist or a hypnotherapist. The specialist is a sort of a coach that leads patients into a trance or a state of relaxation. During this trance-like state, the specialist can make suggestions that can help the patient be more open to change or alter their behavior.

There is no reason to be afraid of the trance-like state. Daydreaming or zoning out is similar to being in a hypnotic state. While the patient is in a high level of focus, they might be more open to certain changes that they would not be open to normally. After the specialist makes their suggestions, the patient will slowly be woken up by the specialist or they will wake up on their own.

However, if hypnosis is done right here is what will happen:

1. The session helps plant different seeds of thought in the patient's mind. These changes will soon start to plant themselves into the patient's mind and continue to grow.
2. The session can also clear the way for the patient to accept the new changes in behavior. It is easier for a patient to accept the new suggestions because normally their mind is so full of clutter that it might be hard to absorb anything new (Legg, 2018).

Hypnosis and Human Reasoning

Research shows that hypnosis is a phenomenon that uses what is known as attentive receptive concentration, and it can even control selective attention at times. Results have proven how attentive reception control works through the process of hypnosis. For instance, during different hypnotic experiments, hypnotists used certain suggestions to alter the participants' perceptions and behaviors.

During hypnosis, suggestions have used on the participant to induce agnosia. This is where the brain is in a certain state that can view what is going on, but the brain cannot recognize other external provocations. It is also known that hypnotism can also influence change in the area of the brain that controls visual partial processing. This is the part of the brain that can identify objects in space and helps them recognize shapes. These occurrences have led to hypnotism being questioned as a valid area of medicine and caused it to be dismissed as a show for magicians.

Those who are amateurs in the field, if not careful, can solicit a different type of attention that can have tragic outcomes if they are not careful.

Those who fall victim to amateur hypnotists feel a sense of anxiety, confusion, and even fear about their experience. For example, in one case, a man was under hypnosis and the hypnotist suggested that he wouldn't be able to find his hotel room because all of the numbers were now written in Chinese. After he was brought out of his hypnotic state, he couldn't find his room for about 25 minutes. He walked around in a panic because all he could see were Chinese lettering on the door. It freaked him out.

In this case, hypnotism was used as a game and the participant didn't know what was going to happen until afterward. His anxiety was at someone else's expense and used for entertainment. It might be amusing to see someone jump on one foot and honk like a goose for a few moments, but to have them experience serious anxiety over a show is a little dangerous knowing that someone has that much power over you.

Another thing that hypnotists can do – that can cause a little bit of anxiety – is known as hypnotic regression or therapeutic regression. This is a valid method that can help people remember some of their memories. These can be memories that they have suppressed and pushed far down for whatever reason, which can cause issues later on in life, or they are memories they might have forgotten and they want to remember. This technique is a way to help psychoanalyze the participant and help them through something traumatic.

Some research has indicated that hypnotic suggestion can also be an effective mechanism in persuading participants to remember things that are fake and convincing them that they are true. These findings shed a negative – but warranted – light on memories and if the memories that are pulled forth are real and not fabricated. Yet, other studies show clear evidence that hypnosis can help others improve their memory, which can differ between each participant.

Reasons to Use Hypnosis and Hypnotherapy

The notion that hypnotherapy can be used to change or alter someone's perception is what makes it a good candidate for a new type of medicinal and therapeutic approach. This alternative approach is used in the United States and Europe to help people with their medical conditions, with their negative habits that impact their health, and even in therapy.

Here are some cases where hypnosis can be useful:

- Helps relieve irritable bowel syndrome (IBS) – Evidence has shown that those who suffer from IBS can benefit from hypnosis to help relieve short-term problems.
- Helps with curing insomnia and sleep disorders – It can be used by counselors and psychologists to help patients manage their insomnia, nightmares, sleep terrors and sleepwalking. In these cases, these specialists will use suggestions in self-control and relaxation to help maintain these conditions.
- Curing migraines – Hypnosis can be used to help treat migraines and tension headaches. The participants that have used it find that it is a great alternative to headache medicine and the side effects that come with taking medicine.
- Pain Control – We are often told that the pain we are feeling is in our head, hypnosis might prove that. It can be used to help those who suffer from clinical pain that they have acquired from surgery and other ailments.
- Quitting Smoking – This is a great way to help those who want to stop with their bad habits, such as smoking, but don't have the will power. "The National Center for Complementary and Integrative Health detail studies suggesting that hypnotherapy may help people who want to give up smoking, especially if paired with other means of treatment" (Cohut, 2017).

- Weight Control - Just like the story at the beginning of the chapter, there is a sense of being able to take control of your life – even on a subconscious level. In this case, the person can be in control of their eating habits and it not being the other way around.

There are three perspective frames that the specialist can use to help change the perspective of the patient.

→ Preframe – Is when the specialist sets the scene before the real event so that the patient sees the real issue
→ Reframe – This is when the specialist helps change how the patient views the current circumstance or event
→ Deframe – This is when the specialist changes how the patient views the event by making it irrelevant

Framing is a great way to help the patient change their behavior because it allows them to get to the core of the problem (the preframe), make them aware of the consequences (the reframe), and then taking away their initial argument because they see it a different way (the deframe).

- Manage Addiction – At this point, the specialist can use hypnosis to help people with addiction manage their problem. They can do this because it helps patients get in touch with their subconscious mind, which is the place where their new suggestions can be planted and continue to grow. Hypnosis can help patients curb their pesky withdrawal symptoms, give them an alternative way to deal with their issues, and give them a drug-free and legal way to escape their problem.
- To Cure Allergies – Studies have shown that hypnosis can help reduce the symptoms of allergies. Using self-hypnosis is psyching

yourself out. For instance, if a person who suffers from allergies focuses their thoughts on environments that are allergy-free. They imagine being on a beach with fresh air or on a mountain covered in snow. It can reduce the symptoms they feel because they are telling their mind they are somewhere else.

- Overcome Sexual Dysfunction – Stress can be a huge factor in not being able to perform. Hypnosis helps patients reduce stress and relax when they're in a trance. The specialist will help the patient using techniques such as focused awareness, deep breathing and visualizing things. There can be personal emotional experiences that can cause sexual problems, especially bad experiences. The art of hypnosis can help because it can make the patient relive the experience, release the pain, shame and/or anxiety that it causes, which then helps lead them to have a better and healthier sex life.
- Help with emotional trauma – Emotional trauma can hurt a person in more ways than they are aware of. It can leave people feeling alone, insecure and even helpless in certain situations. Through the use of regression, hypnosis can help manage this problem by having the patient relive the experience again so that they can fully experience the trauma and learn to heal it.
- Help with depression – Traumatic events that the patient might have experienced can be triggers for depression. They can start feeling depressed because someone they loved died, a lot of bad things happened in their lives like a divorce, loss of their home or even their job. The way that hypnosis helps is by having the patient subconsciously deal with the event. They have to face it and discuss what the event is doing that causes them to be depressed. It can take some time because depression can be very severe.
- To overcome and manage OCD/ Anxiety – OCD stands for Obsessive-compulsive disorder, which can be found in your thoughts

and your behaviors. Many things can cause OCD. However, the most common reasons are genetics, the result of damaged neural pathways, or as what happens the majority of the time, emotional or developmental issues. Hypnosis works in this case, again, because it goes straight for the subconscious mind where regression is used to take the person back to when they noticed first signs of OCD. This helps them find the root cause, showing them that the reason it started no longer exists.

- Stress management and fighting phobias and fears – Hypnosis is another way to help with these three things that are closely related. The specialist has the patient focusing on their underlying emotions that feed into their stress and keeping it in the front of their mind. Regression can be used here to have the patient figure out when stress, in general, started to become the problem. Once they can figure out the reason, they became stressed, or where the fears started, they can start addressing the issue and then realize that those reasons no longer have power over them (Hypnosis Training Academy, 2017).

Chapter Ten: Reverse Psychology

"Reverse psychology is defined as a method of trying to make someone do what you want, by asking them to do the opposite and expecting them to disagree with you"

-James, 2018

This is a strategy that is used by people to get what they want by asking or demanding what they do not want. Scientists use another term: self-anticonformity because your demand goes against what you want.

Another way that psychologists explain reverse psychology is through the term *reactance*. It is referring to the uncomfortable feeling that people get when they feel that their freedom has been threatened. The normal way to respond to that threat is to the opposite of what has been demanded of you. It's the going against authority aspect.

Examples of Reverse Psychology

Reverse psychology is prevalent in many different types of professions because it can help people get what they want, and it can be productive, as well as successful if executed right. For instance, some techniques in sales are based on this very principle, such as the Door in the Face technique. We have all fallen victim to this. Let's say that you are in a used car lot trying to buy a car. The salesman gives you this outlandish price that you would never consider paying. You want to buy the car, but you do not want to pay that much. So, you make a counteroffer for less. This is exactly what the salesman wants. You get the smaller price and the salesman makes the sale, which was his goal in the first place - putting you in a car.

The tactic can also be used in marketing. Here is an example of a store that sells high-quality merchandise. Most of the time, when we go shopping, we see advertisements and the name of the store on the outside of the store. We know where we are going. Well, what if the high-end store has no signs or ads on the outside of the store. It just looks like a regular building. You would have to know where the store was or have been there before to know that they did sell clothes. We all know that this indicates that the retailer is not trying to sell to just anyone. This enhances the mystery of the place and it makes it an exclusive venue. Those who do not want to be excluded or those who are comfortable with the exclusivity will want to buy from the store.

This is a tactic that can be used for good as well. For instance, a parent might use it to get their kid to eat their broccoli. We all know the story; the parent tells the kid to eat their vegetables because they are good for them. But the kid doesn't like them and won't eat them. It is like a constant battle. So, what does the parent do? They use this tactic by getting the kid to want to eat them. How do you they do that? Haven't you ever bought some sweets that you didn't want the kids to eat. You put them in the fridge and tell the kids that those belong to you and not to touch them? What happens? The kid finds a way to eat sweets because they can't have them. They're yours. Why not try that tactic with the broccoli? See how fast the kid jumps on those because they can't have them. We always want what we can't have.

Using this tactic in relationships can be a bad thing if the person using the tactic is trying to get something at the expense of their partner. For instance, you asked your partner to go to the store. But instead of asking them directly, you tell them that they cannot handle the traffic right now. They might go just to prove you wrong. If this becomes a normal occurrence, your partner might stop trusting what you're saying to them, become angry with you and start to believe that you are trying to manipulate them to get what you want. This could backfire because they might believe what you say and start becoming dependent on you.

So, does reverse psychology work? That depends on the people involved. First, the victim has to believe that the culprit wants them to do something before they react to their demands and do quite the opposite. And, if they are aware that you are using this tactic on them, then it is never going to work. But just like persuasion, manipulation, and deception, some people are more susceptible to reverse psychology than others.

Who can fall victim to reverse psychology?

Anyone can fall for any of these tactics because no one is safe from those who will do whatever it takes to get what they want from others. With this being said, those personalities who are more relaxed and laid back don't usually fall for reverse psychology techniques.

So, who does fall more easily for reverse psychology tactics?

Those personalities that are more irritable, stubborn, and overly emotional will find that they fall for these tactics easier than others. Children are more susceptible as well because the cognitive parts of their brains have not fully developed yet. They might not perceive social cues that others can because they are less aware of what is going on. As they get older into their teen years, they might be able to sense what is going on, but they are also at the time in their lives where they are trying to be more independent. However, they do still have a strong urge to fight against authority and might do the opposite of what is asked of them just in spite of that.

How to use reverse psychology

It might sound simple, demand the opposite of what you want. However, here are some steps for you, just in case.

1. Your victim needs to have at least heard of both options.
2. Argue against the option that you want
3. Use nonverbal communication to back up what you are saying because it will make your case stronger.

Just like the other tactics discussed in this book, reverse psychology can be dangerous – especially if the victim finds out what you are doing, and if the motives behind it are wrong. With that being said, it can be used for good – as shown above in the parent example. If you decide that you are going to use it, you should be careful and now what you are doing first, as well as knowing the consequences of using the strategy. Sometimes a more clear, concise and direct approach could be better.

Chapter Eleven: Brainwashing

Brainwashing is a tactic that we hear often. We are told that television commercials bombard us with what to buy, and we are exposed to people's rants on television, radio, the newspaper, online, and social media. These rants tell us what we should look like, what we should be eating, reading, voting for, wearing, etc. We are all subjected to the art of brainwashing on a daily basis and the amount of brainwashing continues to grow.

Before the creation of social media, we were still exposed to social media. However, they would only market to their target audience. If they weren't meant for you, they would be ignored until the next commercial or show came back on the air. For example, you wouldn't have paid much attention to a Polly Pocket or Barbie commercial unless you were a ten-year-old girl or someone who might buy the product for their child.

But things are not like that anymore. Advertising has moved past gender roles, and with the inception of social media, advertisements are now personally geared for us. These websites take information that we provide them. For instance, Facebook uses our likes, comments, status updates, etc. to find the perfect things to advertise to us. They are utilizing brainwashing techniques in the 21st century.

The History of Brainwashing

The term first appeared in the 1950s when Americans were deathly afraid of the spread of communism like it was a poisonous disease. This was the time of the Korean war and there was an extreme belief that Chines Communists had found a way to mysteriously and effectively change the behavior of their prisoners of war.

However, most of the time when we in the modern world hear about brainwashing, we often think about religious cult groups. These groups take people from their families and isolate them, deprive them of sleep, and expose them to loud and repetitive chanting and singing. It didn't seem like there was a lot of torture involved in this type of brainwashing. Rather their minds were controlled by love and what they thought they were receiving from these groups which are things they were not receiving back at home.

Psychologists refer to brainwashing as thought reform, which falls in the category of social influence. "Because brainwashing is such an evasive form of influence, it requires the complete isolation and dependency of the subject, which is why you mostly hear of brainwashing occurring in prison camps or totalist cults" (Layton, 2019). In these instances, the brainwasher must have complete control over those who they are brainwashing. That means that all of the brainwasher's patterns: eating, sleeping, using the bathroom, and other human needs are based on the will of the brainwasher. The brainwasher has a process that they have to complete to make sure that they have exerted ultimate control. They break down their victim's identity so that they do not have one anymore. They then slowly replace the previous identity with a whole new set of behaviors, attitudes, and beliefs that work in their new environment.

Brainwashing Techniques

During the Korean War, the American POWs went under a series of attacks on their sense of self, which is what changed their identity and their personal beliefs. This is the process that they experienced:

- Assault on identity – This is an attack on everything that the person thinks they are and their belief system. The brainwasher keeps denying everything that the victim is and attacks them for days, weeks, months and even years until they break down from exhaustion, confusion, and disorientation. At this point, they start to wonder if what they thought about themselves is even true.
- Guilt – They make the victim feel remorse for anything they had done big or small. Anything that the victim believes is criticized, to how they eat, what they are wearing, and how they look. This makes them feel a huge sense of shame about themselves to the point that whatever they do is wrong.
- Self-betrayal- Now that they question who they are, and they feel extremely guilty, the brainwasher will have the victim agree that they are a bad person. The brainwasher forces the victim to deny his friends, family, and peers who share the same views as them; through physical and/or mental force. The actual action of betrayal to the people that they once felt loyal too, magnifies their sense of shame, as well as their loss of identity.
- **Breaking Point** – The victim starts to have an identity crisis that reaches their mental breaking point. They start to question who they are, and what they are supposed to do. The victim could start losing their hold on reality because they do not understand who they are anymore and what is happening to them. This is when the brainwasher steps in and starts to tempt them with a new identity and belief system that will end their misery.

- **Leniency** – The next step in the process is called leniency, which is a sense of salvation. Now that the victim is in crisis mode, the brainwasher comes in and offers a sort of reprieve, kindness from the suffering and abuse that they have been facing. They might offer something to eat or drink, ask about their home and what they might miss. This seems huge at this point because of all they have suffered. The victim starts to feel a sense of relief, and even appreciation for their offering.
- **Compulsion to Confess** – This is when the brainwasher turns the manipulation around and tells the victim that they are the ones who can help themselves. This is a time where the victim is faced with not only the guilt of pain of their identity crisis, but they also feel the relief of the leniency that was offered by the brainwasher. Now, they start feeling a desire to return the kindness that was just offered them, and they start to think of the possibility of confessing their sins to relieve some of the pain and guilt they feel about themselves.
- **Channeling of Guilt** – After going through months of assault that has led to confusion, personal breakdown and moments of leniency from the brainwasher(s), the victim feels guilt but they do not know what it is for. This is where the brainwasher comes in to remind them of what they have done wrong and connects the guilt to the victim's old belief system. This is where they are lead to believe that the new belief system is something good and all of the pain, and agony is related to the old belief that they are holding on too.
- **Releasing of Guilt** – The victim now knows that there is a chance they can release their guilt. They attribute their guilt to the old belief system, and they can escape the guilt. All they need to do is denounce all of the people and institutions that are associated with their old identity and belief system. Then they can release all of their pain. Once the victim rejects all of his old self, this is when the

brainwasher comes in to offer them the new belief system and identity to follow.

- **Progress and Harmony** – Now the brainwasher is there to help the victim rebuild themselves. The new identity and belief system is introduced as good. All of the abuse stops, and the victim is offered a sense of physical comfort and mental calm if they start believing the new system that was placed in front of them. However, the victim is given a choice or made to believe that they are given a choice to choose between their old self or possible new self. The new identity that they are being offered is safe because it not like the one which led to their breakdown.
- **Final Confession and Rebirth** – At this particular point in the process, the victim is ready to choose their new path, belief system, and identity. The old belief system is rejected because it does not offer the peace and security that they get with the new one. The victim is now inducted into the new system through a set of rituals or ceremonies because they are now reborn.

The process of brainwashing and mind control is not only devious, but it is dangerous and harmful to those who are involved. It is stripping them away from everything they are to further someone else's agenda. It can be scary to think that people can influence a person's mind that way.

Chapter Twelve:Dark Psychology and the Power of Seduction

"Seduction is not about the culmination or gratification of desire; it is about the thrill of the desire itself. It is the game that is played as the desire comes closer, and closer, and closer, and being able to maintain that tension of wanting for a long, long time"

Madsen, 2012

Seduction has nothing to do with sex. It is the opposite of sex because sex occurs when our desires are actually met. Seduction and anticipation go hand in hand. It is about extending the pleasure of doing things by waiting for them.

However, even though seduction is the art of chasing your desires and waiting for them to come to you – to build a type of happiness. It is also very manipulative and cruel because it is about process and persuasion. It is seen as a game though because it is never really one-sided. The start does involve one person, which is commonly known as the male in the role of subjugator and the other who reacts submissively. There is a certain level of mutuality in this game because the submissive one does have to consent.

Now, just because there is consent given doesn't mean that it cannot be harmful when it is at its worst. Remember, this game is based solely on the two individuals who are playing along. In itself, seduction can be oppressive, enough to put someone to shame. It can be considered demanding and even threatening and coercive at times. At times it is captivating, alluring and enticing. And even though the game is never started with consent on both sides, it always ends up that way.

After the game is played and the consent is given, the seducee often feels a sense of regret because seduction does not prey on the logical self, but the impulsive, spontaneous, romantic self. It is often the case that the seducee views their submission (consent) as a personal weakness on their character. They caved and gave in the desire of the seducer. They have realized that when they have been seduced and the lovemaking is done that the seducer didn't love or care about them at all. Instead, they had been used to gratify the seducer's sense of self.

This is why it is important to know what you are doing if you are going to seduce someone. Otherwise, it can go horribly wrong. Here are a few tips to consider when practicing the art of seduction:

- Choose the right person – This is about the hunt, and the one thing that a hunter does is study their prey and choose which one shows a sign of weakness because they allow for a perfect chase, which is what the game is all about.
- Create a false sense of security – Do not make yourself obvious because you might be too direct or scare them away. Let them become aware of you by introducing yourself through a third party or create a neutral relationship that can move gradually from friend to lover.

- Mix up your signals – You don't want them to know that you are blatantly interested. Instead, you need to see if they are interested as well. So, throw out different signals by showing a few of your cards, but not much. Just enough to indicate that there might be some sort of interest there.
- Be desirable - You don't want them to think that you are desperate and that they are your only option. Instead, you want them to think that you are being desired by others in the vicinity. They will start to become vain when they see that they are the object of your attention

Of course, these are just a couple of steps that you can use to start your seduction plan. You want to make sure that they show some sort of interest before you continue to move on with the game. Otherwise, it is just a big waste of time.

Just understand that with these few steps, you can see how manipulative the game can be and how it can be dangerous to those who do not have a high level of self-esteem. So, if you tend to find yourself on the receiving end of the seduction game, be careful because you never know how much that person will harm you after the chase is over.

Chapter Thirteen: How to Use Dark Psychology in your Daily Life

People use psychology within their daily lives, so why not use Dark Psychology and the tactics to protect yourself in everyday life. There are quite a few personality traits that can be very harmful if you get caught up in them. Sadists fall under this category. For instance, this personality type enjoys inflicting suffering on others, especially those who are innocent. They will even do this at the risk of costing them something. Those who are diagnosed as sadists feel that cruelty is a type of pleasure, is exciting, and can even be sexually stimulating.

We do have to face the fact that we manipulate people and deceive people all the time . When it comes to deception, people are deceiving not only others on a daily basis, but they are also deceiving themselves. People often lie to gain something or to avoid something. They might not want to be punished for an action, or they might want to reach a goal, and they self-deceive to get there.

Here are some examples of how people can deceive themselves:

Having a hard time studying - this is a common occurrence. When people are trying to study, they find a lot of things that can distract them, especially cell phones and social media apps. They will find just about anything to distract them from the task at hand. These types of people seem to have a phobia of not studying long or well enough and they are afraid that they will come home with a bad grade and it will show how unintelligent they are. So, they take the art of self-deception and come up with the idea that will help prevent them from studying. This excuse will weigh better in their mind if they do end up getting a bad grade on their test. The person's subconscious is telling them that it is better for them to get bad grades for lack of studying than to study and failing and therefore having to blame their intelligence. They couldn't live with that.

Here are other ways that we regularly deceive ourselves:

- Procrastinating – People often waste time when they do not want to study or do something important. However, the main reason for procreating could be the phobia against failing and procrastinating was just an excuse. Self-confidence can be an issue as well.
- Drinking, doing drugs and carrying out bad habits -People often fall into bad habits, drink, or do drugs just to have something to blame if they fall again. This type of person will try to convince themselves that if they could stop doing drugs, they could be very successful. When they are the ones deceiving themselves and standing in their own way.
- People often hold back because life is unfair. They tell themselves that we all live in a big lie that most people believe in, but not them. It is easier to blame it on life being unfair, then hold ourselves accountable for not reaching our goals.

If you realize that you have been deceiving yourself, here is a couple of things that you can do to change that.

- Remember that you are smart and the fact that you have been able to deceive yourself reaffirms it. If you were not smart, there would have been no way that you would have been able to come up with some of those ideas.
- It is important to learn how to face your fears. If you are running from a certain trauma, or not wanting to take a test, you have to remind yourself that you are stronger than this and that you can beat it.
- Lastly, once you face your fears, your self-confidence and courage will grow.

Manipulation in our daily lives

Manipulation is an underhanded tactic that we are exposed to on a daily basis. Manipulators are people who want nothing more than to get their needs met, but they will use shady methods to do so.

Those who grew up being manipulated, or being around manipulation, find it hard to determine what is really going on because if you are experiencing it again, it might feel familiar. Maybe you were manipulated in a previous relationship, or the current relationship that you are in reminds you of your childhood.

This is important because manipulation tactics break apart communication and break a person's trust. People will often find ways to manipulate the situation and play games rather than speaking honestly about what is going on. However, others value communication only to manipulate the situation to reveal the weaknesses of the other person, so that they can be in control. These types of people do this often in conversation. They have no concern with listening to others talk about anything about themselves. And they are not there to help those people get through whatever it is that they are going through. It is all about dominance in this case and that's it.

Here are some of the tactics that can be used on an everyday basis:

. Some of the common techniques that we can experience are:

- **Lying** – White lies, untruths, partial or half-truths, exaggerations, and stretching the truth.
- **Love Flooding** – Through endless compliments, affection or through what is known as buttering someone up.
- **Love Denial** – telling someone that they do not love you and withhold your love or affection from them until you get what you want.
- **Withdrawal** – through avoiding the person altogether or giving them the silent treatment.
- **Choice Restriction** – Giving people options that distract them from the one decision that you don't want them to make.
- **Reverse Psychology** – Trying to get a person to do the exact opposite of what you want them to do in the attempt to motivate them to do the direct opposite, which is what you really wanted them to do in the first place.
- **Semantic Manipulation** – Using common words with a person and later telling them that you have a different view of the conversation that you just had.
- **Being Condescendingly Sarcastic or Having a Patronizing Tone** – To be fair, we are all guilty of doing this once in a while. But those who are manipulating us in conversation are doing this consistently. They are mocking you; their tone indicates that you are a child, and they belittle you with their words.

- **Speaking in Universal Statement or Generalizations** – The manipulator will take the statement and make it untrue by grossly making it bigger. Generalizations are afforded to those who a part of a group of things. A universal statement is more personal.

→ Example: Universal Example: You always say things like that.
→ Example: Generalization: Therapists always act like that.

- **Luring and Then Playing Innocent** – We, or someone we know, is good at pushing the buttons of our loved ones. However, when a manipulator tries to push the buttons of their spouse and then act like they have no idea what happened. They automatically get the reaction that they were after and this is when their partner needs to pay close attention to what they are doing. Those who are abusive will keep doing this again and again until their spouse will start wondering if they are crazy.
- **Bullying** - This is one of the easiest forms of manipulation to recognize. For example, your spouse asks you to clean the kitchen. You don't want to, but the look they are giving you indicates that you better clean it or else. You tell them sure, but they just used a form of violence to get you to do what they wanted. Later they could have told you that you could have said no, but you knew you couldn't. It is important to note that if you fear that you cannot say no if your relationship without fearing for your safety, then you need to leave the relationship.
- **Using Your Heart Against You** – Your spouse finds a stray kitten and wants to bring it home. The logical thing to do would be to discuss being able to house and afford the cat. But instead, they take the manipulative approach. Their ultimate goal is to make you feel bad about not being able to take care of the animal. Don't let anyone, even your spouse, make you feel that you cannot make the best choice for

you. You do not have to take care of the kitten if you don't want to. Bottom line. Meet their manipulations with reasonable alternatives.

- "**If you love me, you would do this"** – this one is so hard because it challenges how you feel about your spouse. They are asking you to prove your love for them by giving them what they want from you, making you feel guilt and shame. The thing you can do in this instance is to stop it altogether. You can tell your spouse that you lovo them without having to go to the store. If they wanted, you to go they could just ask.
- **Emotional Blackmail** – this is ugly and dangerous. The idea that someone will harm themselves if you leave them is harmful at the core. They are using guilt, fear, and shame to keep having power over you. Remember that no one's total well-being is your responsibility alone. You have to tell yourself not to fall for it. This will always be a manipulation tactic. However, you can tell them that if they are feeling like they are going to harm themselves that you will call an ambulance to help them.
- **Neediness When it's Convenient** – Has your spouse started to feel sick or upset when they didn't get what they wanted? This is a direct form of manipulation. For instance, they don't want to go somewhere with you and have a panic attack, that you have to help them through, so that they don't have to go at all. This is not healthy at all, and if this persists you should think about ending the relationship.
- **They Are Calm in Bad Situations** – When someone gets hurt, or their conflict, somebody dies, your spouse always seems to not react with any feeling. They are always calm. This type of manipulation makes you think that perhaps how you are reacting is a bit much. Maybe your emotions are a little bit out of control. This is a controlling mechanism because no one should be able to tell you how to feel. This might seem like they are questioning your mental health and

maturity level, and you find yourself looking to them and how to respond in certain situations. If this something that happens often and you see that you keep falling for it, you might need to go and see a therapist. This way, they can help you work on your emotional responses and find your true feelings again. This manipulation method can be very damaging to your psyche. At the moment, learn to trust your gut. It will not steer you wrong.

- **Everything is a Joke** – This is a two-part manipulation tactic. Your spouse will say hurtful things about you, and then when you get upset, they get upset because you can't take a joke. Other times they will joke about you in front of others, and if you don't respond positively, you are again ruining the fun. This is a way to put you down continuously without having to take responsibility for it. Remember that you are not ruining the fun here, but you have to stand up for yourself.
- **Forcing Their Insecurities On To You** – Your spouse will manipulate you into thinking that their insecurities are now your problem and will use them in a way to control you. They will tell you that they have been cheated on before, and that's why they don't like that you have male friends and that you should stop. Or they use them when they act a certain way, controlling your behavior because they don't want to lose you. When it comes to this situation, you have to find a balance. You can care for someone and make sure that you are considerate of their feelings, but you should not be manipulated into feeling what your spouse wants you to feel. Their manipulation is ruled by guilt.
- **Makes You Responsible and Accountable for What He/She Feels** – This manipulation tactic is quite funny because your spouse spends a great deal of time making you think and feel like you cannot think about your or their feelings on your own, but that you

have to be reminded of how they feel. They tell you how you feel, and then you are responsible for how they feel. If they're sad, you made them sad. You must have done something to make them feel that way. This tactic belittles you also because they take a lot from you and tell you how you feel, but then they want you to be responsible for how they feel.

- **Makes You Want What They Want, and Makes You Believe That Too** – We all make compromises in relationships. However, what is not normal is having to put aside what you want completely to appease your spouse so that you can fully commit to what they want. If you soon start to see that your spouses' needs are being met far more often than yours, you need to start questioning things. You need to ask yourself if you are giving them what they want because you want to, or because they made you feel guilt or a sense of responsivity for how they feel? If you find that you are giving up everything for them, then you need to reconsider what is actually important.

When determining how to get away from those who manipulate you, it is important to know your fundamental human rights and how you should not be treated.

You have the right:

- To be respected and treated with respect.
- To express how you feel, your opinions and the things you want and need.
- To set your own priorities and goals.
- To say no and not feel guilty about it.
- To get what you pay for without guilt or shame.

- That it is okay to have an opinion that is different from those in the group.
- To stand up for yourself.
- To take care of yourself.
- To protect yourself from being threatened or harmed psychically, mentally and emotionally.
- And, to create your own life full of happiness.

These specific rights help you set important boundaries that will help protect you in the future. We do have to remember that there will be people in this world who do not respect these rights or us as people, just things they can use to move on to the next phase. Do not let others take you over and manipulate your life. You are the only one who has power and authority over your life. And you are the only one who is in charge of it too.

Keep your distance from those who you think are trying to manipulate you or others. See how they act when they are around different people in different situations.

Avoid blaming yourself, even though it is common to feel that way when someone is trying to expose your weaknesses and use them for their personal gain. You have to keep telling yourself that you are not the problem and that they are trying to get you to surrender your power. If this occurs, ask some very basic questions: is my spouse treating me with respect? Are they reasonable with me? Do I feel good about myself while in the relationship? And, finally, is this relationship going two ways or one?

If you answer negatively to all of these questions, then you know that you are not in a good relationship because you are going to continue to keep being manipulated from someone who tells you that they care, but they don't. Once you realize that, you will be better off.

Manipulation can be a tactic that you are not aware of until someone points it out or you start connecting the dots. Often, people figure it out when they are already stuck in a situation that is dangerous to get out of. With this being said, try to get to know people before you invest time in them. This is easier said than done because people don't usually reveal their true nature, especially those who mean to do you harm until you have already invested a lot of time with them. If you find that you feel uncomfortable and start to question what is going on. You should listen to your gut and move on. Everyone deserves to be happy.

Conclusion

The notion that Dark Psychology is prevalent and that it is part of our world can be a scary thought. People have centered their whole lives around using these tactics, whether at work or home to get people to do what they want and to harm them. Within this book, we broke down the components of manipulation, persuasion, deception, and brainwashing and how you can avoid those who mean to do you harm.

Those who suffer from narcissism, Machiavellianism, and psychopathy suffer from mental diseases that can be harmful to their loved ones as well as their friends. Not all of these people harm others intentionally. However, some do, with or without the excuse of feigning a mental illness diagnosis.

We defined Dark Psychology at the beginning of the book and indicated that it falls into the same category as general psychology. However, it goes deeper into the human mind and helps pinpoint tactics that people use to motivate, persuade, manipulate, and coerce to get what they want from others.

The Dark Triad is a term in Dark Psychology that can be helpful when trying to pinpoint the beginning of criminal behavior.

- Narcissism exhibits these traits: egotism, grandiosity, and lack of empathy
- Machiavellianism uses a form of manipulation to betray and exploit people. Those who practice this do not practice morality or ethics.
- Psychopathy is a trick to those who put their trust in these types of people. They are often charming and friendly. Yet they are ruled by impulsivity, selfishness, lack of empathy, and remorselessness.

None of us want to fall prey to manipulation, persuasion, deception, reverse psychology, brainwashing, or even hypnosis, especially from those who we love. The unfortunate truth is that we often are. Dark Psychology tactics can be used regularly to harm us for perverse fulfillment of others.

The fact that people can be used as pawns on a chessboard makes all of us want to understand Dark Psychology more and to figure out what it is, and how we can save ourselves from it. This book was written as a guide that provides a list of tactics within each chapter so that the reader would know how to educate themselves on the devious actions of others and how they could go about protecting themselves.

Knowledge is a key element in protection because the more you know, the more you can read behind the devious acts of others within your life or who you find trying to coerce you into purchasing something that you didn't need.

Out of all of the methods we discussed in this book, the art of hypnosis has been used by medical science for something good. There are many ailments that hypnosis can make better or even cure. And we are not just talking about mental ailments, but physical as well. Hypnosis can be used to help cure some of the side effects that are caused by chemotherapy and radiation in cancer patients.

We all know that there has been a lot of skepticism for this alternative medicine due to the quacks that use it as a laughingstock. However, when used correctly, this type of medicine can greatly benefit people because it wakes the subconscious up to letting go of things that they are holding on to that might be causing a plethora of problems in their lives.

With this being said, all of these methods can be used for good, it is just based on their intentions and the overall outcome. Those who use manipulation tactics do not use them for the intention of helping anyone. Manipulating is changing someone's thoughts, actions, and behaviors to fit someone else's (the manipulator's agenda). There is no way to sugarcoat some of these techniques.

And that is why they fall under the Dark Psychology umbrella because they have been used by criminals to get what they want as well.

We hope that you have used this book as a sort of guide to help you understand these methods and be able to spot them, as well as have a list of tactics that can be used in order to help you protect yourself in the future.

Because we all know that someone is going to try to make us a victim of one of these methods in our lives, and I for one would want to be as ready as I could possibly be.

References

Cerejo, L. (2018). The Ethics of Persuasion. *SmashingMagazine.* Internet. Website. Retrieved from https://www.smashingmagazine.com/2018/06/ethics-of-persuasion/Cohut, M. (2017). Hypnosis: What is it, and does it work? *Medical News Today.*

Internet. Website. Retrieved from https://www.google.com/amp/s/www.medicalnewstoday.com/articles/amp/319251Hogan, K., & Speakman, J. (2013). Psychological Tactics & Tricks. *Gulyani.com.*

Internet. Website. Retrieved from https://www.google.com/amp/gulyani.com/covert-persuasion-psychological-tactics-tricks/amp/James, A. (2018). Reverse Psychology: What Is It, And Does it Work? *Betterhelp.*

Internet. Website. Retrieved from https://www.betterhelp.com/advice/psychologists/reverse-psychology-what-is-it-and-does-it-work/Legg, T.J. (2018). Is Hypnosis Real? And 16 Other Questions, Answered. *Healthline.*

Internet. Website. Retrieved from https://www.healthline.com/health/is-hypnosis-realLouv, J. (2014). 10 Ways to Protect Yourself from NLP Mind Control. *Ultraculture.*

Internet. Website. Retrieved from https://www.google.com/amp/s/ultraculture.org/blog/2014/01/16/nlp-10-ways-protect-mind-control/amp/(2012). 20 Most Common Manipulation Techniques Used by Predator.

Noggle, R. (2018). Why the difference between persuasion and manipulation matters?

FastCompany. Internet. Website. Retrieved from https://www.fastcompany.com/90212788/why-the-difference-between-persuasion-and-manipulation-matters/ Nowicki, D. (2016). 'Daisy Girl' political ad still haunting 50 years later. *Azcentral.* Internet. Website. Retrieved from https://www.google.com/amp/s/amp.azcentral.com/amp/15233151Roberts, M. W. (2019). The Difference Between Persuasion and Manipulation. *Michael W. Roberts.* Internet. Website. Retrieved from https://www.michaelwroberts.com/content/persuasion-manipulation/

(2017) What Can Hypnosis Treat? 15 Common Issues Resolved by Going Into A Hypnotic Trance (PLUS Scientific Studies to Back It Up). *Hypnosis Training Academy.* Internet. Website. Retrieved from https://www.google.com/amp/s/hypnosistrainingacademy.com/what-hypnosis-can-treat/amp/Yetter, E. (2017). Top 10 Unbelievable Cases of Hypnotism from The Past. *Listverse.* Internet. Website. Retrieved from https://www.listverse.com/2017/09/09/top-10-unbelievable-cases-of-hypnotism-from-the-past/

CPSIA information can be obtained
at www.ICGtesting.com
Printed in the USA
LVHW101545220321
682097LV00041B/1914